ELDERS' TRAINING

THE WAY
TO CARRY OUT
THE VISION

BOOK 3

WITNESS LEE

Living Stream Ministry
Anaheim, CA • www.lsm.org

First Edition, December 1985.

Library of Congress Catalog
Card Number: 85-82042

ISBN 0-87083-116-X (hardcover)
ISBN 0-87083-194-1 (softcover)

Published by

Living Stream Ministry
2431 W. La Palma Ave., Anaheim, CA 92801 U.S.A.
P. O. Box 2121, Anaheim, CA 92814 U.S.A.

Printed in the United States of America

06 07 08 09 10 11 / 10 9 8 7 6 5 4 3

CONTENTS

FOREWORD

During February of 1984 over three hundred and fifty brothers from six continents gathered in Anaheim, California with Brother Witness Lee for a two week international elders' training. The messages that were released at that time are the contents of this four volume set. Book one presents the essential aspects of the ministry of the New Testament; book two sets forth the vision of the Lord's recovery; book three covers the way to carry out the vision; and book four emphasizes other crucial matters concerning the practice of the Lord's recovery.

Those of us that were in these meetings were deeply convicted of our need to be further enlightened by the Lord concerning God's economy and concerning the intrinsic essence of the New Testament ministry which is for the carrying out of this divine economy. As the Lord's recovery is continually spreading throughout the world, these messages are more than crucial and urgently needed. We believe that they will render a great help in preserving all the saints in the central lane of God's economy, without any deviation, for the fulfillment of His eternal plan. Our hope and expectation is that these messages will become a governing and controlling vision for all in the Lord's recovery. May we prayerfully consider all the points presented in these books and accept them without any preferences.

November, 1985   Benson Phillips
Irving, Texas

CHAPTER ONE

THE NEED TO ACQUIRE
THE CRUCIAL POINTS OF THE TRUTH
AND A BIRD'S-EYE VIEW
OF THE SCRIPTURES

In this chapter, we want to begin to fellowship on another item which I consider quite great, that is, how to carry out the ministry. In Book two we covered the vision in the Lord's recovery. Now we must see how to carry out the vision. This is altogether an experiential matter. We may be able to relate quite much to doctrine and visions, but now we must see the way to carry out what we have seen. Concerning the vision, undoubtedly, the written Word is our base. This is also our track to follow and our rule to be under. The way to carry out the vision, however, is our practice. Paul told Timothy to commit the things that he had heard from him to faithful men who would be competent to teach others (2 Tim. 2:2). Although this verse does give us some way to carry out the vision, it is still a principle. We still need to know how we can become competent to teach others. Because we cannot see many details in Paul's word in 2 Timothy 2:2, I feel the best way to fellowship this matter is to check with our own experience.

PICKING UP THE CRUCIAL POINTS OF THE TRUTH

In the United States, we have over twenty years experience in this matter of teaching. According to my experience and observation, we must first pick up the crucial points of the truth to carry out what we have seen. There is no basic truth that can stand by itself as a single, all-inclusive point. The truth is mainly composed with many points. For instance, consider the great truth of salvation. This one item contains many, many points. We must pick up these points and get ourselves into them.

Even a Life-study message cannot stand on one point alone. It is at least composed with a few points. If you want to get into a Life-study message, you must first read it in a general way. By reading it in a general way you will be able to realize that some points are more crucial than others. You must, first of all, pick up the crucial points and get into them.

Understanding the Vocabulary

Also, in reading anything we must first understand the vocabulary. If you read the Chinese Bible, you must understand the Chinese language; if you read the English Bible, you must understand the English language; and if you are trying to read the Greek Bible you must understand the Greek language. No one is capable enough to remember every definition of a word. I do not think that even Webster himself could remember all the things in his dictionary. If you could check with him on the meaning of a certain word, he would probably say, "Let me open the Webster's dictionary to see." This shows us that to get into the truth we must have a good lexicon. You should not think that your English is so good that you do not need a dictionary. This still is not adequate. You may be adequate only to a certain degree. I have always considered myself only adequate to a small degree even in my mother tongue of Chinese. None of us are adequate enough to know the full, proper, and accurate definition of any word. Even those of you who have a master's degree in English cannot explain a word exactly and adequately unless you go to the best lexicon.

Another problem among all the languages of the world is that the same word has different denotations. The dictionary may give you five denotations for the same word. When a particular sentence uses a certain word, you must have the discernment to realize which denotation of this word to apply. If you do not have a proper understanding, you will apply the wrong denotation.

In the outline of the Recovery Version of Mark, I used the

word "initiation"—the initiation of the Slave-Savior. Before I used this word, I had a great amount of consideration. Mark begins neither with the birth of Jesus nor with His genealogy. Luke begins with the conception and birth of Jesus. Following this Luke gives us the genealogy of Jesus. Mark, however, begins with the initiation of the Slave-Savior. The word initiation here actually means the same as the word inauguration. Some may say this is inauguration, but how can a slave be inaugurated? It is fitting to say that there is an inauguration for a president. How, though, can a slave be inaugurated into his slavery? This shows that the word inauguration is not suitable to the context. The thought here is the Savior's coming into His duty, commission, or service. It is awkward, of course, to say "the coming in of the Savior." Finally, I decided to use the word initiation.

The Chinese translators of our Recovery Version endeavored and worked very hard and I appreciate this. However, they translated the word initiation into Chinese according to the first denotation in Webster's dictionary, that is, "the beginning." To initiate, to begin, something is one meaning; but to initiate a person into a particular club or organization is another meaning. When a person is initiated into a new group, that means the person is being brought in, introduced, or conducted in. In the book of Mark it is not the beginning of the Savior, but the Savior's being brought in, being introduced, being conducted in. In our translation of the Bible, we should never put something out in a light way. This shows us that we may pick up a point concerning the truth, but understand it absolutely in the wrong way and thereby miss the mark. Not only do we miss the mark by doing this, but we make a big mistake. This shows us again that it is not so easy to study the Bible.

Even to study the Life-study messages and the notes is not so easy. Sometimes it took me more than an entire day to compose just one crucial phrase in the notes of the Recovery Version. This does not mean that I was sitting at a desk for twenty-four hours working on this phrase. But while I was doing things throughout the day, my heart and my mind were considering that phrase. I had to invent some expressions to communicate the spiritual things the Lord has shown us. Language comes out of culture. A new culture needs a new language, and new points in the culture need new vocabulary. In the entire history of human culture there have never been so many items, not only in the general spiritual field but even more in the field concerning how we are one with the Triune God. Many points in this field are foreign to human culture. Therefore, the human language does not have the vocabulary because there is not something corresponding to it in the human culture.

By His mercy, in the Holy Spirit and in our spirit we experience something which has never existed and been understood in human culture, so there has never been the kind of vocabulary to express this experience. When I wrote the notes, therefore, I had to invent new terminology. In our fellowship concerning the vision in the Lord's recovery of the church I was forced to create the adjectives "Christly" and "resurrectionly." I did the same thing in 1971 in Elden hall in Los Angeles when I said that we needed to be "Jesusly human." If we say that we need to be human like Jesus, this is imitation. This kind of expression bears a wrong denotation. This is like saying a monkey should be like a man. As a result, we invented the term "Jesusly human." We needed a new adjective which did not exist in Webster's dictionary or any other English dictionary. We should not say that such a term is wrong because no one has ever used it before. We must see that in any culture new words must be invented as the culture is progressing and new things are transpiring. It is easy to read two or three lines of the notes of the Recovery Version without realizing that in these lines there are some crucial points which took me one week to express and compose. Therefore, to read the Bible and to read a proper interpretation of the Bible is not so easy.

I found out that a number of brothers and sisters read the Life-study messages as they would read a newspaper. We must realize that there are also some newly composed phrases in the Life-study messages. The expression may be common, but what is conveyed in the expression is not so common. In the Recovery Version of Romans I did not have the time to compose an extensive note on the word "designated" in 1:4. There are a number of messages, though, which have been given on the matter of the designation of Christ and of our experience of designation. (See messages 2 and 52 through 56 of the *Life-study of Romans*.) The word designation may seem common to you, but the point is not common. When you read a message on Romans with the matter of designation in it, you should dwell on this point. Do not let it go. Sometimes you need to dwell on one point for two days. Even to pick up one point of the truth is not a rough, light, easy, or quick matter. Many times when the brothers and sisters read the Life-study messages they do not practice this principle— to learn how to pick up the crucial points.

Eloquence versus Utterance

I hope you would also give me the freedom and the mercy to say something frankly and honestly to you all. Since I have been in America over twenty-two years, I have noticed that most of the Chinese are far inferior in speaking in comparison to the Americans because of the different educational principles in their cultures. Most American children learn how to speak and the mothers check on their speaking. The Chinese are the opposite. Even in their schools they do not train people to speak. The Americans may know only five percent, yet they can speak ten percent. The Chinese may know ten percent, but they cannot speak five percent. When I was listening to the testimonies in the meetings concerning the Life-study of the Bible, I noticed that the American saints are very smart in picking up funny thoughts many times, but they neglect the crucial points. They say things to make everyone laugh, but there are not crucial points to impress people. One brother said that every time he listens to my speaking, he always feels that I do not have the eloquence. However, this brother testified that after I was finished speaking, something of life and the Spirit had gotten into him.

In Ephesians 6:19 the Apostle Paul charged the saints to pray for him that he might have the utterance, and in Colossians 4:3 the apostle charged the saints there to pray that God would open a door of utterance. This word in the Greek for utterance is *logos,* the word. Speaking in the spiritual realm is not a matter of eloquence but a matter of utterance. It is possible that a person may be able to speak quite well and eloquently and still impart nothing. Another person may utter things in an awkward way, but in his awkward speaking the Spirit is ministered (2 Cor. 3:6). This is the biblical utterance, the logos. This is a word which is not for good listening, but a word that conveys "a diamond" to others. Public speakers are trained not to repeat too much, but in the ministry we are not concerned for the rules of public speaking. In the ministry we are serving people with Christ. When you speak, you must believe that the Spirit is speaking with you. You must follow the Spirit's feeling as to whether what you have spoken has been really taken and received by the audience. Sometimes you may have repeated something twice already, yet in your spirit you have the realization that you did not get through on this point. Therefore, you do not save your "sermon" and you do not care for your good speech. You must care for the presenting of the "diamond" to people.

Sometimes the mother in a family must repeat herself many times to get the food into her naughty child. Many times I must repeat myself because of your "naughtiness." I realize that the "naughty boys" did not get it. I do not care for good manners. I only care for my children getting the food into them. Many times in our past we sat under a very trained, educated, and eloquent pastor but after his speaking we went home with nothing. For the last ten years, however, many of you have been sitting under a kind of speaking which is awkward and repetitious, but when you go home you have the realization that an injection got into you which heals and nourishes you. In our reading of the Bible we must also take this way. We must repeat our reading to take care of a certain point repeatedly. In like manner, when you get into the printed pages of the Life-study, you should not pick up funny thoughts. You must pick up the crucial points.

Realizing the Crucial Points

I told the saints a number of times that in their corporate

pray-reading of the Word they should not make fun or pray with funny thoughts to make others laugh. This means nothing and despises the meeting Spirit. We are pray-reading in the presence of the Lord, and even with the Lord inside of us. How could we pray in a "playing" way? This is wrong. In the same principle, in reading the pages of the Life-study messages, we must learn how to realize the crucial points. For example, when there is a message telling us that Jesus Christ was designated the Son of God we must consider what it means for Him to be designated. We must pick up this crucial point because today we are the same in principle as the Lord. He was there as a man in the flesh with the name Jesus. We also are men in the flesh, but within us we have the Son of God. According to the flesh Jesus is out of the seed of David, but according to the Spirit of holiness Jesus was designated the Son of God. We also need to be designated. Do not think that only Jesus needed the designation. Today all His believers in Him need the same kind of designation.

In my messages on Romans I mentioned clearly that this kind of designation of the Lord Jesus should also be our experience. Designation is actually our sanctification. Sanctification is to live out the Lord. Therefore, designation is to let the Lord live out of us. When He lives out of us, this living out is His designation. Now we can see that this is not just a doctrinal, objective point of theology that has nothing to do with us. According to the flesh our Lord is out of the seed of David, but according to the Spirit of holiness He is designated the Son of God. Theology would merely tell us that this shows that Christ has two natures—one according to the flesh and the other according to the Spirit. According to the flesh, He is the Son of David and according to the Spirit, He is the Son of God. This is very much like today's theology. The seminary graduates are trained and taught in this way yet they never applied these things to themselves. The Apostle Paul, however, was not that way and we should not be that way. In Paul's very opening words in the book of Romans he laid a foundation of sanctification. Even Jesus needed the sanctification, the designation. Therefore, we must learn that when we read a proper exposition or commentary of the holy Word, we should not read it as a newspaper. We must pick up the crucial points.

A BIRD'S-EYE VIEW

Second, after picking up the crucial points, we must put these points together. In order to have a "bird's-eye view" over a message, a chapter, or over a portion of the Word, we must learn how to put the points together to make a section. For example, there may be twenty-five points in a certain chapter of the Bible, but you must learn how to section this chapter. This chapter may not be a single section, but it may be composed of five sections. Not knowing how to section a chapter is like writing without punctuation, without spaces between sentences, and even the more without spaces between words. If there is no space between words and sentences, it is hard to understand what is being said. In the ancient Greek manuscripts of the Bible there is no space between words and sentences and even no punctuation. The scholars who put out the modern form of the manuscripts spent much time to decipher the word, sentence, and paragraph divisions. There is still some argument as to whether some words go at the end of a sentence or at the beginning of another sentence. In the same way, if we do not know how to section a chapter, we cannot know or understand it. This is like writing a long sentence without any space in between the words.

Many of us who read the Bible and the Life-studies pick up some points but we do not relate any of these points to other points. You may have the realization that the first seven points of a chapter are the components of one section. Sectioning a chapter in this way gives you a clear view, a bird's-eye view, of the entire chapter. Then this bird's-eye view gives you more light through the points you have picked up. First you pick up the main points and after sectioning these points you have a bird's-eye view. When you look at all the sections, this will increase your light and increase your vision. This makes the entire chapter more meaningful. This is not an easy task. This requires you to become conversant with all the verses and crucial points. To section a book or to paragraph a chapter requires that you have a basic, governing, ruling, controlling, and directing knowledge of the entire Bible. Otherwise, your sections and your paragraphs will be according to your natural understanding. It may be quite possible that your section is against the principle of the writing of the holy Word. This is why I do not encourage the young ones among us to go to so many other books. A number of expositions do not give the proper sections of the books. Their sectioning is even somewhat against the principle of the writing of the holy Word. As a result of taking this sectioning, you can be misled.

The Outlines, the Notes, and the Cross-references

In our studying of the Recovery Version there are three subsidiary items to the text itself: the outlines, the notes, and the cross-references. The notes are very crucial, but I doubt that many of you realize that some of the outlines are more crucial than the notes. I would not say that the cross-references are crucial. I would only say that they are helpful. First, in reading the Recovery Version you must learn of the outline. The outline is the first crucial item. I could write a note on any verse of the Bible within one day, but I cannot finish the writing of the outline of a book like Romans within one day. When you outline the book of Romans, its entire sixteen chapters must be in front of you. You must have a full understanding of its contents and every crucial point should have been impressed into your understanding. Then you will be able to make very good sections for an outline. Please do not excuse yourselves by saying that you are not scholars or experts. I am speaking to all of you who are elders, who are taking the lead in the church meetings, and who are taking the lead of certain groups. You must equip yourself with the holy Word. I was told when I was young that when some were asked to give a sermon they would use the Scofield Reference Bible. They would pick a word such as "sanctified" and use the chain reference to trace this word's usage in the Bible. They used this chain reference to make a sermon. This never enlightens or nourishes people. We must be equipped with the holy Word.

A Bird's-Eye View of a Chapter, of a Book, and of the Entire Bible

To become rich, we need to pick up the points, we need to have a bird's-eye view of a chapter or of a section, and we also need a bird's-eye view of the entire book. Finally, we need an ultimate practice—to have a bird's-eye view of the sixty-six books of the Bible. Then the entire Bible means something to you. We need to progress from the single items of the truth to knowing the outline of a section or of a chapter. From this we need to see the outline or the bird's-eye view of an entire book. Finally, from the outline of a book we must have a bird's-eye view of the entire sixty-six books of the Bible. When you reach this point, a good foundation will have been laid with all the basic principles to govern, to direct, and to rule your interpretation of any word, any verse, any chapter, or any book of the Bible. You are not only safeguarded but also very much enriched.

You may say that this is hard, but I do not think so. This, however, takes time. You should not read the Bible and the Life-studies in the old way. Whenever you pick up the Bible or the Life-study of any book of the Bible, you must read them in this way. You must pick up the single, crucial points and have an outline of a certain chapter or a certain section. Then you must progress to have an outline of the entire book. After finishing a book you should not go ahead. You must go back to make an outline of this book. Try to do this. This is the basic way for you to carry out the ministry. If you do not have such a basic way, it will be hard for you to speak. Even to learn a language you must learn the alphabet, the spelling of certain words, and then you must learn more words. Then you must learn how to compose a single sentence and progress further to composing a paragraph with five sentences. You must learn the grammar of the language and more vocabulary. Gradually, this kind of knowledge will be constituted into your being. Then you will speak and write the language spontaneously and fluently. You have the capital to do it. Some Chinese immigrants who come to the United States speak with broken English. Instead of saying, "One dollar and twenty-five cents," they may say, "One dollar two-five cents." Many of today's Christians read the Bible in the same principle. They read by using the spiritual, broken language. They do not have the basic knowledge of the spiritual language since they never were educated this way. This is why I want to present to you the proper way of how to carry out the ministry. The truths must be constituted into your being. Then you can carry out the ministry.

Even in the playing of basketball, the players must practice what the coach teaches them until this practice gets into their being. Then without any intention and without any thought they can execute the plays and the moves out of their very being. Then they will win the game. After much practice, they have the inner sense of what to do and of how to handle the ball. Please do not say that to study the Bible in this way is not easy. Many of us have been in the Lord's recovery for at least fifteen years, but we did not get much of the proper help. This is one of the reasons why we called this urgent gathering. I believe that through our fellowship some help may be rendered to you. If you would pick up this fellowship and go back to practice every day, you will see the difference after only half a year.

CHAPTER TWO

A BIRD'S-EYE VIEW OF MARK AND ROMANS

The best way to become impressed with a book of the Bible
and to keep this book in your memory is to keep the bird's-eye
view of this book. Once you become impressed with a bird's-
eye view of a book, this book remains in you. In this chapter,
we will look at the bird's-eye view of the book of Mark and of
the book of Romans.

THE BIRD'S-EYE VIEW OF MARK

I must honestly tell you that in my whole Christian life I
never loved the book of Mark until I was forced to write the
notes on this book for the winter training of 1983. At least one
of my old Chinese Bibles contained outlines of nearly all the
books of the New Testament. This Bible, however, did not con-
tain an outline for the book of Mark. I did not make an
outline for this book because I did not think it was worth it.
Before preparing for the winter training of 1983, the only
thing that I could tell you about the outline of the Gospel of
Mark is that in the beginning of the gospel of Jesus Christ,
the Son of God, John the Baptist came out (1:1-4), and at the
end the disciples went out to preach the gospel to all the creation (16:15, 20). Even though there was no incentive to write
this outline and even though I did not have much to write, I
was forced to write something to match the writing of the
other books. Therefore, the Lord helped. After such a writing,
I got a clear bird's-eye view of the book of Mark. I have been
deeply impressed with this view especially after the writing
of the notes, the outline, the message outlines, and even more
after speaking something concerning these sixteen chapters

in the training. I do not think it would be so easy for me to forget what I have been impressed with.

Mark gives us a full portrait of how Jesus as the slave of God serves a sinner. I do not say sinners because all the pieces in this book should be considered as a collective case. Do not consider Peter's mother-in-law as an individual person sick of fever. She is a part of the sick person. Do not consider the leper as a separate individual. He also is a part of one complete sick person. In other words, the book of Mark shows us a complete sick person who was sick of fever (1:29-31), sick of leprosy (1:40-45), sick of paralysis (2:1-12), and sick of a flow of blood (5:25-34). This is a four-fold sickness. In the entire book of Mark you cannot find a fifth sickness. You may ask concerning the one with the withered hand (3:1). That case does not show the person who was sick; it only shows one of his members being sick. For example, with the blind the eyes are sick, with the deaf the ears are sick, and with the dumb the mouth is sick. However, the entire being, the entire person, is sick of only four kinds of diseases according to Mark—fever, leprosy, paralysis, and the flow of blood, the issue of blood.

After the healing of the entire person, there is the exposure of the real inner being, the heart, in chapter seven (vv. 1-23). The heart is seen in chapter seven as something that is dirty and contaminated with nothing good and nothing pure. This is the inside, real situation and condition of such a fallen and sick person. The one who is sick of fever, leprosy, paralysis, and the flow of blood is rotten, dirty, and contaminated within his heart. Then this dirty inside was cleansed. Following this is a case of feeding—the feeding of the children and the pet dogs (7:27). Accompanying this sort of feeding are two miracles of feeding—the feeding of five thousand (6:30-44) and the feeding of four thousand (8:1-9). We must see that in this Gospel there are at least three feedings. The small miniature feeding is the feeding of the pet dogs. The Syrophoenician woman was considered in the eyes of God as a pet dog. The unbelieving Gentiles are the wild dogs, while all the chosen Gentiles are the pet dogs. We should praise the Lord that we are not wild dogs, street dogs, but we are pet dogs under the table of the children, who are the Jews. We cannot compare with the Jews, but, praise the Lord, we are still the pet dogs under the table eating the children's crumbs. Preceding this miniature feeding is the feeding of the five thousand, and following it is a confirmation of this feeding which is another feeding of four thousand.

We should not consider Peter, James, and John as individuals in the bird's-eye view of Mark. You have to consider that they are part of the same person. This person was healed from his fever, cleansed from his leprosy, recovered from his paralysis, and rescued from his issue of blood. He was exposed in his inner being and he was fed. It is this kind of person that can go up to the mount of transfiguration (9:2-13). A person sick with fever or sick of leprosy could not go up the mountain. Only such a person who passed through this marvelous process is qualified to go up to the mount of transfiguration.

This person was healed from all his diseases, cleansed from within, and fed. At this point this person is healed, made alive, and cleansed inside, but he is still deaf, dumb, and blind. At this point what this man needs is a listening ear to be able to listen to the heavenly speaking (7:31-37). This is so that he will not speak nonsensically any longer. He speaks nonsensically because he never hears (7:32). He needs the healing of his ears to hear clearly. Then he needs the healing of his mouth to be able to speak properly and the healing of his eyes so that he can see. It was on the mount of transfiguration that the need of the healing of the listening organ, speaking organ, and seeing organ began. When you were healed from the general diseases, were made alive, and were fed, you were able to go with the Lord to the mountain of transfiguration. Now you need to see and you need to hear the heavenly voice. You need to see that Christ is unique and that He is the unique replacement to replace everything, including you. Do not propose the building of three tabernacles the way Peter did on the mount. There is not one tabernacle for the law, one for the prophets, one for Christendom, or one for human culture. We must hear Him and we need such a hearing ear to hear Him. Do not hear culture;

do not hear the prophets; do not hear the law; do not hear Moses or Elijah; do not hear anyone. You hear Him. Then from Mark 9 the Lord began to unveil who Christ is, what Christ will do and go through, and where Christ will be (9:30-32; 10:32-34). This is the basic teaching from chapter nine to the end of this book.

From Mark 9 onward Jesus brought His disciples with Him to bring them into Himself, to bring them into His death, and to bring them into His resurrection. To get into Christ you must go through His death and resurrection. Then you will reach Him. By this we can see how wonderful this book is.

In the first few chapters of the book of Mark, it seems that the Lord Jesus did not grasp Peter, James, and John. In the last four or five chapters, however, the Lord did grasp them. They were there with Him wherever He went and whatever He did. Even Peter's mistakes and shortcomings did not stop the Lord from grasping him until the Lord Jesus brought him to the cross with Him. Do you realize that when Jesus died on the cross Peter was there? Jesus went to the cross with Peter. Probably Peter did not realize this, but he was brought there (Gal. 2:20). Jesus brought Peter and the other disciples into His death, into the tomb, into His resurrection, and into His ascension. Therefore, Peter and the others eventually became absolutely in Jesus Christ. Then they could carry out Jesus' commission. Now all of them are able to do what Jesus did in chapter one. In chapter one there is only one Jesus, but in chapter sixteen there are many reproductions of Jesus.

Here is a full portrait of a person sick of fever, leprosy, paralysis, and an issue of blood. Such a person was dying but he was made alive, he was healed of all his diseases, he was cleansed within, he was fed, and he went up to the mountain with Jesus. However, he still needed to hear, to speak, and to see, so Jesus healed all the organs related to these functions (7:31-37; 8:22-26; 9:14-29; 10:46-52). Now this person began to hear the voice from the heavens, to speak the proper thing, and to see the vision. Jesus brought this person into His death (15:16-41) and into His resurrection (16:1-18) and this person ascended to the heavens in Jesus Christ (16:19). Then this collective person came down to preach the gospel just as Jesus did (16:20). This is a bird's-eye view of the entire book of Mark. This is not merely a history or a story but the divine significance of Mark.

Now we come back to these four kinds of diseases. We must realize that every person is abnormal. Everyone has a fever. It may be that everyone's temperature is one hundred and five degrees. When a wife gets mad with her husband or when a husband gets mad with his wife their temperature goes up to one hundred and ten degrees. Every descendant of Adam is abnormal with a fever. Everyone is also sick of leprosy; they are unclean. Also, everyone is paralyzed and cannot walk. They cannot do anything before God. Finally, everyone is flowing blood, dying, leaking life. Was not this your case?

We cannot be represented by one case. The Lord Jesus needed four gospels, and we need four "gospels" too. Our "gospels" are negative gospels. He has four sides and we have four sides too: one side is abnormality, another side is that we are dirty and contaminated, a third side is that we are paralyzed, not able to walk or do anything, and the fourth side is that we are leaking life. We are not living, but we are dying. The case of the woman with the flow of blood is merged with the case of a girl who died at twelve years of age (5:21-43). Her death is at the end of the twelfth year of the woman's flow of blood. This indicates that the flow of blood issues in death. We were abnormal persons, dirty, unclean, paralyzed and dying. However, the Slave-Savior, the Slave of God, came to render us a service. He healed us and He saved us from our sick condition. We were healed from all our diseases, cleansed from within and fed by the Lord. We became a pleasant person like Peter, James, and John. We all were qualified to go up the mountain but we got there blind, deaf, and unable to speak. We were healed and made alive, but we still did not have the seeing, speaking, and hearing ability. We needed the further healing of our organs. At this juncture Jesus was transfigured before them and Christ was unveiled because by this time they were healed in their hearing and seeing organs. They could hear and they could see so the Lord brought this

collective person all the way to the cross and entered into resurrection and ascension.

This is not an allegorization. It is impossible for anyone to
allegorize things so rightly. What we have done is to put the
jigsaw puzzle pieces together to enable us to see a full picture
of the Slave-Savior serving the fallen sinners with His all-
inclusive salvation. We need such a bird's-eye view of every
book of the Bible.

THE BIRD'S-EYE VIEW OF ROMANS

The bird's-eye view of the book of Romans is mainly of four
stations. You must remember and be impressed with these
four stations. Romans is composed of sixteen chapters with
four sections of four chapters each. The first four chapters end
with the word justification (4:25); this is the station of justification. From chapter five through eight is the section on
sanctification. The third section, from chapter nine through
chapter twelve, is on the Body of Christ. Finally, the last
section is a station ending with the local churches because
the churches are mentioned in chapter sixteen (vv. 1, 4-5). If
you have such a bird's-eye view of these four stations you can
see that the book of Romans shows us the fallen condition of
a sinner who is going to be made a son of God that he can be
an organic member of the Body of Christ which is expressed
in the local churches. This one sentence covers the entire book
of Romans from chapter one through chapter sixteen with the
four major stations.

Justification

The first section goes from the fallen stage of the sinner
through God's condemnation according to the law. Then
Christ's redemption redeems us from God's condemnation.
Finally, this redemption brings us God's justification through
our faith in the Redeemer. This is the first section of the book
of Romans.

Sanctification

The second section of the book of Romans begins with
chapter five. As a justified person from chapter five you must

realize that first you are in Adam, but now you have been transferred out of Adam into Christ. You are no longer in Adam but in Christ. Also, since you are in Christ, you are in union, identified with, His death and resurrection, and you are in His death and resurrection (6:4-5). Because you are no longer a natural person in Adam but a resurrected person in Christ, you should no longer live in the old flesh (Rom. 7). You must live in and according to the Spirit (8:2, 4, 6, 13). Thus, you are sanctified not only positionally but dispositionally. You are not merely outwardly justified with God. This only changes your outward condition. Now you have been transferred out of Adam into Christ and in Christ through His death and resurrection you are being transformed. This transformation is a subjective, dispositional sanctification. Through this sanctification, we are fully conformed to the firstborn Son of God as His many brothers and as the many sons of God (8:29). You were once sinners in Adam, but now you are here in Christ, sons of God and brothers of Christ, to be conformed into His image. This is the dispositional and subjective sanctification, which actually is transformation and also the proper designation. We are all designated to be the sons of God and the members to compose the Body of Christ.

The Body of Christ

The third station of Romans brings us to the Body of Christ. This section begins from chapter nine and shows us that it is altogether a matter of God's mercy in choosing us (9:11, 16). It is not up to us. We have been redeemed, justified, transferred into Christ, and here in Christ we are transformed, sanctified, and fully designated as sons of God to be members of Christ to form His Body and even to be conformed into His image. This is altogether a matter of God's mercy, of His merciful choice. Thank the Lord we were all chosen and that it was not up to us. Then in chapter ten we see that as chosen ones to be the vessels of mercy unto glory (9:23), we must call on the name of the Lord for our enjoyment of His riches (10:12). He is rich unto all that call upon His name. This is quite meaningful. We were chosen by His mercy, but we must enjoy Him by calling. We must be a caller. We must call on the name of the Lord that we may enjoy all of His riches. In chapter eleven we can again see the thought of God's mercy—all things are out of Him, through Him, and unto Him (11:36). Everything is up to Him and we as the Gentiles are the wild olive branches grafted into the genuine olive tree (11:17). This is out of Him; this is through Him; and this is unto Him. This is altogether God's business, God's doing. It is not of us. The only thing which we can see that we have to do in these sections is to call upon the Lord's name. First, you believe in Him and then you call on Him. This will bring you to the station of the Body of Christ.

We must be deeply impressed with this section—that it is altogether of God's mercy and of God's doing. He will have mercy upon whom He will have mercy. He will show His compassion to whom He will show His compassion. Also, everything is out of Him, through Him, and unto Him. This indicates that it is altogether His doing. We have been grafted into the genuine olive tree and here in the tree we are enjoying all the juice of the root of the fatness of the olive tree. The juice of the root refers to the riches of Christ which we can enjoy by calling on His name. By this we reach the station of the Body of Christ.

The Local Churches

From chapter thirteen through chapter sixteen we are shown how to live in this Body. In other words, we are shown how to have the church life. To have the church life we must live according to chapter thirteen. According to chapter thirteen we must keep a good and proper relationship with the government (13:1-7), we must love others (13:8-10), and we must awake from our sleep to be a living person watching and waiting for the coming day (13:11-14). We must live this way. Then in chapter fourteen we see that we must live the church life by receiving all the saints (14:1). We must be careful about this. This is a deciding factor as to whether our meeting is sectarian or not. It all depends on how we receive the saints. We must receive the saints without any kind of division. This means that we must receive all the saints—whoever God has received we must receive. We should not say that we do not like a certain brother because he is not according to our taste. If we do not receive a brother and keep him outside the door of the church because he is not "our kind of Christian," this is sectarian. We must receive the ones who are weak in their belief.

According to Romans 14 some are so weak that they do not dare to touch the sacrifices to the idols. An idol is nothing and the things offered to the idols are nothing. A weaker believer, though, may not be able to eat these things because his conscience is so weak. He may still keep a religious diet, not eating the things which are unclean. He would not even touch the sacrifices to idols and he may not want to break the sabbath. It does not matter how weak this believer is, however, you must realize that as long as he is a real brother you must receive him. He is your weak brother. Do not blame him. You have to blame the Father who begot him. The Father has accepted him. Who are you to exclude him? To exclude him would make you sectarian and the people you meet with a sect.

Chapter fourteen also tells us that the church life is the practice of the kingdom of God. The kingdom of God is not eating or drinking, but righteousness, peace, and joy in the Holy Spirit. (See Romans 14:17 and note 17^1 in the Recovery Version of Romans.) The church life as the practice of the kingdom goes in three directions—one direction is with yourself, another direction is with others, and the third direction is with God. The kingdom of God is righteousness toward yourself, peace with others, and joy with God in your spirit. A church life which is a practice of the kingdom of God is in these three directions. Chapter fifteen goes further to tell us that we must receive the believers according to Christ (15:7). We must be what Christ is and we must do what Christ does. Then we see that the entire church will be sanctified and offered to God for His satisfaction (15:16). Finally, in chapter sixteen we see the proper local church as the expression of the Body of Christ. In Romans 16 we see the local churches and the saints living in the living church. If you live in Cenchrea you must be a member of the church there (16:1). If you live in Rome, you must be a member of the church in

Rome (16:5). Other churches are also mentioned in chapter sixteen (vv. 4, 16).

This fellowship should give us a clear, bird's-eye view of the book of Romans. John and Revelation are also good illustrations of other books of which we need a bird's-eye view. We need to acquire a bird's-eye view of every book in the New Testament.

CHAPTER THREE

NOT BECOMING CONTENTED

A LESSON FROM CHURCH HISTORY

Based upon what we have picked up by the crucial points and by the bird's-eye view over an entire book and even over the entire Bible, we must learn how to go further based upon what we have read and studied. Church history shows us that throughout the centuries many Bible readers and teachers became contented once they got something really good from the Bible. They were not only satisfied with what they had, but they became contented and they became full. As a result, there was no more capacity in their being, so they became proud. They were stopped from going further, and they would not go on. You may have a bird's-eye view of Matthew, Mark, Luke, John, Acts, and Romans. You may know all the crucial points in these books and you may even have a bird's-eye view of the entire Bible. At this point you may have the attitude that you know the Bible and, thus, you would not go any further.

Church history tells us that at certain times God raised up and initiated some of His lovers into a new realm. They began to doubt the religious traditions of their day and they began to see something further. The Reformation is an illustration of this. About a century before Martin Luther's time, the Lord raised up a certain environment that forced some of His seekers to realize that they were short in their vision and practice of what was contained in the divine revelation of the holy Word. Therefore, they began a new age and they were initiated into a new realm. They began to see. After Luther's time, however, the Protestant churches stopped seeking further.

The Lutheran churches and the state churches in Northern Europe held the belief of justification by faith, but these Protestant churches were mostly stopped from seeing anything further. Then there were many others who began to see things from the Bible, but the things that they saw were not in the central lane of the New Testament ministry. They began to see baptism by immersion, the presbytery, and the brotherhood of all the believers. Some others began to see some deeper things such as sanctification, but even they never got a proper, full, and thorough view of the Biblical sanctification.

Under the leadership of Zinzendorf there was a partial recovery of the church life in Bohemia. He was the first one to see something higher than the others, but still this was not adequate. Then the Brethren were raised up under the leadership of J. N. Darby and many precious Bible truths were unveiled. They saw something further, but they did not see the emphasis on Christ as life. They also never touched in a thorough and definite way the identification of Christ with the Holy Spirit. They knew Christ mostly in an objective way. They saw much more and went much further, but they did not call people's attention to Christ as life and to Christ as the Spirit. They also talked about the church mostly in an objective way. They did not see the crucial, subjective aspects of the church, which include the church as the fullness, the new man, and the lampstand.

Later, thousands of missionaries went to China. Their teaching became shallow and superficial because they thought most of the Chinese people were not educated or knowledgeable. The missionaries had to establish schools to teach the Chinese. They even taught them their native language of Chinese so that they could be helped to read the Bible. Many of the missionaries at that time thought that the Chinese language was not adequate for the translation of the Bible. Even the Brethren held the attitude that in their "home assembly" they practiced faith in the Lord for their living; however, when they went to China they said that the Chinese people were not qualified to live by faith. Among the Brethren Assemblies in China, many of the British brothers were living by faith, but the Chinese preachers and "Bible women" were paid by the Brethren since they considered that the Chinese were not qualified, equipped, or able to live by faith. Also, when they taught, they taught in a low way. They lowered down their teaching purposely because they considered that the Chinese people could not understand the higher and deeper truths. They held the concept that they were superior. We should praise the Lord, however, that some among them were really men of God. They were not satisfied with this kind of preaching nor with this kind of attitude. They prayed very much.

I was born and educated in Christianity. I studied in a Christian school established by Americans and directed by an American principal. A number of us brothers, including Brother Nee, knew Christianity and were educated by Christianity. The Lord caught us and we began to investigate. Through much study we found that many of the things that we heard were superficial. Brother Nee took the lead to investigate the Bible teachings and to get into the depths of the Bible. He discovered that there were a lot of books written which were much deeper in their content than what we had heard. He began to buy many books and we were all influenced by him to buy many books concerning church history and the truths of the Bible. Then we presented everything in our mother tongue of Chinese—what the missionaries called the "native dialect." As a result, we uplifted the preaching with a higher kind of Bible interpretation and we presented the higher and deeper truths. Then we expounded the Bible. This shocked many of the missionaries. They could not understand how native Chinese could expound the Bible in such a profound way. Some of them were convinced and turned to the way of the Lord's recovery.

Because western Christianity had become more than contented, this kind of situation forced the Lord to do a new thing. Every denomination was contented. Even nearly every missionary was contented. Not many were seeking. But the Lord sovereignly created a kind of environment to raise up some "natives" to begin a new period of time. It was really new. We began to see new things from the Word. Actually, this was just a new understanding of the old, even ancient Bible.

Actually this was nothing new. What we saw were old, ancient things already contained in the Bible, but to our view it was new. I relate this because I am concerned that you younger ones, after picking up the crucial points and the bird's-eye view of the chapters, sections, books, and of the entire Bible, will become contented. Do not do this. All the things we have presented to you in the ministry are just "openers."

ISAIAH 9:6

Even after I opened up some portions of the Word, I studied them further. I would like to illustrate to you what I mean by sharing with you what I have seen from a further study of Isaiah 9:6. Many of you know that I have been speaking on this verse for over twenty years in America. I did some further study on this verse and I believe that I have seen a better way to present it. I spoke quite much in the past that Isaiah 9:6 shows us that the Son is the Father. We also put out a number of publications containing this truth. After all these publications, I began to realize that I must present the truth in Isaiah 9:6 in a very basic, biblical way. The very basic, biblical principle is to interpret any verse by taking care of the context of that chapter. Then you need to take care of, in a further way, the context of the entire book. This is still not adequate. It is finally necessary to take care of the context of the entire Bible. This is a basic word concerning the basic principle of interpreting the Bible, that is, that every word of the Bible needs the entire Bible to interpret it.

Isaiah 9:6 has become a great debatable verse mainly due to the Son being called the Father versus the traditional theology of the Trinity always remaining in three distinct and separate persons. The best theology says that the Trinity is three distinct persons, while the poor theology says that the Trinity is three distinct and separate persons. Traditional theology keeps the three persons in a distinction and separation. According to this theology, you should never say the Father is the Son and the Son is the Father and the Son is also the Spirit. If you say this you will be immediately condemned as modalistic. Modalism, of course, is a serious heresy and a serious condemnation is ascribed to it. In order to avoid being condemned as modalistic, no interpreter or teacher of the Bible would say that the Son, having been called the Father, is the Father. No one would dare to say this. Whoever would say this would be condemned.

We young brothers in China, however, were faithful to tell the truth, not caring for being condemned. I came to the United States and dared to tell people that the Son is the Father. Then the opposition was aroused and some condemned me of being modalistic. Even some among us took the side of the opposition. They said that the everlasting Father in Isaiah 9:6 is not an accurate translation because in Hebrew everlasting is a noun. Therefore, the proper translation should be "the Father of eternity." Based upon this, they said that the Son is called the Father of eternity and that this does not mean that the Son is the Father in the Godhead of the Trinity. The Father of eternity to them is not the Father in the Godhead of the Trinity. This is another Father. They said the Father of eternity is like George Washington being called the father of the United States or like Thomas Edison being called the father of electricity.

Many believe in this way because for them to remain in the traditional theology with the understanding of three distinct and separate persons, they need some refuge. Many traditional theologians stay in this refuge of interpreting Isaiah 9:6 by saying that this verse does not refer to the Father in the Godhead but to the Father of eternity. Jesus as the Creator surely is the Father of eternity. It is quite reasonable to say that Christ as the Son of God was the Creator of everything. However, for the traditional teachers to indicate that besides the Father in the Godhead there is another Father is a top heresy. This is the reason why we put out a booklet titled, *What a Heresy—Two Divine Fathers, Two Life-giving Spirits, and Three Gods*. This was published in a major California newspaper, but no one answered it. This was a challenge which defeated the traditional, theological interpretation concerning the Triune God. No one answered this article because they could not answer. Many Christians were caught in the heresy of two divine Fathers, two life-giving Spirits and three Gods. This is the unconscious, subconscious belief of today's traditional theology.

By the Lord's mercy I have been strong not only to preach but also to insist that we do not have two divine Fathers, two life-giving Spirits and three Gods. We only have one God who is the Father, who is the Son, who is the Spirit, and who is the Triune God. This One is the Creator. This is our God as revealed in His holy Word. He is the Creator, He is the Father of eternity, and the Father of every family in the heavens and on earth (Eph. 3:14-15). Paul in his preaching to the philosophical Greeks in Acts 17 told them that they were the offspring of God (vv. 28-29). Since God is the Creator, the Source, of all men, He is the Father of them all (Mal. 2:10) in a natural sense, not in the spiritual sense as He is the Father of all the believers (Gal. 4:6) who are regenerated by Him in their spirit (1 Pet. 1:3; John 3:5-6). Also, in James 1:17 we see that God is "the Father of the lights." Many Christians understand the lights in this verse to mean spiritual lights or divine lights. However, lights here refer to the heavenly luminaries. The Father is the Creator, the Source, of these shining bodies. Our God is not only our Father who begat us with His divine life, but also the Father of all the heavenly luminaries such as the sun, the moon, the stars, and the planets. He is the Father of all the heavenly bodies since they all were created by Him. This does not mean that this Father who is the Creator of all things is not the Father in the Godhead but another Father. Isaiah 9:6 has been debated in such a way. Some say that the Father of eternity in this verse is not the Father in the Godhead. I have considered many times what the best way would be to present Isaiah 9:6 as a rebuttal to this interpretation. In order to do this we must be brought back to the basic principle of interpretation, that is, to take care of the context of the chapter, of the entire book, and of the entire Bible.

Based upon this, I did some further study of Isaiah 9:6 based upon the context of Isaiah. The book of Isaiah refers to God as Father two other times. Isaiah 63:16 says, "For thou art our Father, though Abraham knoweth us not, and Israel doth not acknowledge us: thou, O Jehovah, art our Father; our Redeemer from everlasting is thy name" (ASV). There are four main points in this verse: the Father, Jehovah, Redeemer,

and everlasting. In this verse Isaiah told us that God is not
only the Son as in 9:6 but also Jehovah. Jehovah indicates
that God is the Triune One, the Eternal One, the great I Am,
the One who is, who was, and who is coming. We must also
have a further realization that Jehovah in the Old Testament
equals Jesus in the New Testament. "Jesus" is the Greek
equivalent of the Hebrew word Joshua (Num. 13:16), which
means Jehovah the Savior or the salvation of Jehovah. Hence,
Jesus was not only a man, but Jehovah; and not only Jehovah,
but Jehovah becoming our salvation. This verse also tells us
that Jehovah, who is our Father, is also our Redeemer. Generally speaking, God is our Redeemer, but strictly speaking
Christ is our Redeemer. Isaiah firstly tells us that God is
our Father and that He is also Jehovah and our Redeemer.
Therefore, this verse indicates that the Redeemer, Jesus
Christ, is the Father of Israel. Actually, the Father of Israel
is also the Father of eternity. This verse, however, does not
stress the Father of eternity but the Father of the people of
Israel. This Father is Jehovah, the Old Testament Jesus, and
Jehovah is the Redeemer, and this name ("our Redeemer") is
from everlasting. Isaiah 9:6 and 63:16 correspond to one
another. If we are going to interpret Isaiah 9:6, we must
come to Isaiah 63:16 in the same book.

In order to get a proper interpretation of Isaiah 9:6 we
must also look at Isaiah 64:8: "But now, O Jehovah, thou art
our Father; we are the clay, and thou our potter; and we all
are the work of thy hands" (ASV). In this verse we see that
Isaiah called Jehovah "our Father." In 63:16 He was also
called by Isaiah "our Father" and "our Redeemer." This name
was from everlasting. Isaiah speaks of God being our Father
three times—in 9:6, in 63:16, and 64:8. We must ask the question—are these three Fathers referring to one Father or to
two Fathers? If you do not say that the Father in Isaiah 9:6 is
the Father in the Godhead, then what about the Father in
63:16 and 64:8. Is the Father in these verses the Father in the
Godhead? In Isaiah 9:6 the Son is called the Father of eternity. To say that the Father of eternity in this verse is not the
Father in the Godhead is wrong based upon the context of
the book of Isaiah. This interpretation cannot stand when we

compare Isaiah 9:6 to the other two references to the Father in the same book of Isaiah.

There are also some other verses in the Old Testament which show that God was the Father of Israel. Deuteronomy 32:6 says, "Do ye thus requite Jehovah, O foolish people and unwise? Is not He thy father that hath bought thee? He hath made thee, and established thee" (ASV). Moses told the children of Israel in this verse that Jehovah was their Father. The thought in the Old Testament is that God was always the Father of the children of Israel. Furthermore, Exodus 4:22-23 tells us that God sent Moses to see Pharaoh and tell him, "Thus saith the Lord, Israel is my son, even my firstborn: And I say unto thee, Let my son go, that he may serve me." Again we can see the thought in the Old Testament that God was the Father of Israel.

Isaiah prophesied in Isaiah 9:6 that a child would be born to us and a son given to us and that this son is called the everlasting Father. The everlasting Father is our Father and also the Father of the children of Israel. To say that the Father of eternity is not the Father in the Godhead is off and not according to the context of Isaiah and of the rest of the Bible. This interpretation is like a foreign article wedged into the body of the Scriptures.

I want to show you young brothers not to be contented merely with what you have learned from the notes of the Recovery Version and from the Life-study messages. For example, for a verse like Isaiah 9:6, I did not interpret it according to the basic principle of interpretation, which is to take care of the context of the book. You should go further to interpret this verse according to the context of the book of Isaiah. I am just illustrating to you that if you study the Bible in this way, you will see something further. I was not contented with my presentation of this verse, so I did some further study according to the context of the entire book of Isaiah, which tells us that Christ, the Messiah, was the Father of the children of Israel. Is not this Father also the Father in the Godhead? I hope we have all seen that the Father of Israel, unequivocally, is the Father in the Godhead.

SECOND CORINTHIANS 3:17

Now we want to see something further concerning 2 Corinthians 3:17. Most of us have probably been contented with our interpretation of this verse. The traditional teachings avoid saying that Christ is the Spirit. They say that the Lord in 2 Corinthians 3:17 does not refer to Jesus Christ, but that it is a general address referring to God. We have argued in the past that according to the context of this section which starts at 2:12, the Lord here must refer to Christ the Lord (2:12, 14, 15, 17; 3:3, 4, 14, 16; 4:5). According to the context of 2 Corinthians 2 through 4 there is no other way to interpret 2 Corinthians 3:17 but to acknowledge that the Lord in this verse is Jesus Christ.

When I studied this verse further, I realized that it is in the functional sense that the Lord is the Spirit. In order to see that what is mentioned in 2 Corinthians 3:17 is a matter of function, we must take care of the context of this verse. Darby indicates that verse 7 through verse 16 of chapter three is a parenthetical section. With this understanding as a basis, verse 17 is a direct continuation of verse 6 which ends with the word "the Spirit gives life." Verse 6 tells us what kind of Spirit the Lord is. He is a life-giving Spirit. Life-giving is a function. Verse 17 also tells us that where the Spirit of the Lord is there is freedom. Freedom refers to the work of freeing. Life-giving is a function and freeing is also a function. Then the following verse, verse 18, tells us that "we all with unveiled face, beholding and reflecting as a mirror the glory of the Lord, are being transformed into the same image from glory to glory, even as from the Lord Spirit." In this verse we see the transforming function of the Spirit. These are the three main functions of the Spirit in chapter three—life-giving, freeing, and transforming. In such functions, Christ today is the Spirit.

This shows us that we should not be contented with whatever understanding we have of the divine revelation. We must realize that the holy Word is not so simple. It is a big mine which no one can exhaust. Even though I have presented something more concerning Isaiah 9:6 and 2 Corinthians 3:17 there is still more concerning these two verses. Who can say that he has exhausted any verse or any point in the Bible? The Bible is too profound.

JOHN 6:57

I want to give you another illustration of how we should never be contented with what we have. In John 6:57 the Lord tells us, "he who eats Me shall also live because of Me." A few hymns in our hymnal tell us that "eating is the way." We must ask ourselves what the eating way is. How do we eat Jesus? In my writings I have only given you a small amount of information on this subject. Because I did not give you an adequate definition of the way to eat Jesus, you must study this point. To fully understand this point you must take care of the entire context of John 6:57. In verse 63 the Lord says, "It is the Spirit who gives life; the flesh profits nothing; the words which I have spoken unto you are spirit and are life." This indicates that to eat Jesus is to receive Him into us as life. This corresponds with the principle of eating. Eating is to receive some organic nourishment into your being as your life. Eating is to take in the life supply. Some might say that it is heretical to say that people can eat Jesus. The Bible, however, says to eat Jesus.

We must realize that to eat Jesus is a figure of speech. It indicates that we need Jesus as our life supply so we receive Him into us as life supply just as we eat food. The Lord uses bread to illustrate that He is the life supply by saying that He is the bread of life (John 6:48). We eat bread by receiving it into our organic body, by digesting it into our blood, fibers and tissue. Therefore, to eat Jesus is to receive Him into our being. He is the Spirit and the Spirit is in the Word, so we have to take His Word by exercising our spirit. Then we receive the Spirit in the Word. This is Jesus becoming our inner life supply. Here we could see the way to eat Jesus.

Chapter six of John also indicates the Lord's death, that is, His being slain. Verse 54 tells us that His blood is drinkable and that His flesh is eatable. Here flesh and blood are mentioned separately. When blood is separate from flesh, it indicates death. This helps us further to see how to eat Jesus. To eat Jesus means to receive the crucified and resurrected

Christ through His Word by exercising our spirit to receive the life-giving Spirit as our life supply.

The way to carry out the vision is by taking care of the crucial points, by taking care of the outline, the bird's-eye view, and by never being contented. Go on and on to further study and further seeking. I hope that you would do this work. Do not wait for me to do it.

CHAPTER FOUR

NOT TEACHING DIFFERENTLY
FROM GOD'S ECONOMY

Prayer: Lord, we worship You for Yourself. We worship You for Your Word. Lord, we treasure You in Your Word. Lord, we thank You for this gathering. We believe it is sovereignly of Your mercy. O Lord Jesus! It is all a mercy that we are here. Thank You that we are under Your mercy. We enjoy Your rich anointing. Thank You, Lord that You have opened up Your Word to us. We are looking to You for this message. Be with us in Your Word. Lord, grant us to see a clear vision and have a clear way to carry out Your vision. Give us the way, Lord. Give us the wisdom how to handle the vision of Your New Testament. Lord, do cover us again. We hate Your enemy. We hate that he is still troubling us in our mentality, in our concept, and in our opinion. Lord, we are still so natural in our soul without much transformation. Have mercy upon us. What we need is Your mercy. Amen.

THE PROBLEM OF MINISTRY

Thus far, I believe we have all been deeply impressed with the need of a vision of God's New Testament ministry. This training is a training on the ministry. Throughout the twenty centuries of church history, the divisions, confusions, and problems which have taken place among all the Christians were all due to a ministry. Whatever you minister produces something. If you minister the heavens, something heavenly will be produced. If you minister earthly things, surely the issue, the coming out, will be earthly. The many divisions and confusions among the Christians today all come from one source—a ministry. The Presbyterian denomination or division came out of the ministry of the presbytery. The Baptist division came out of the ministry of baptism by immersion. All the different kinds of Christian groups come out of different ministries. A ministry is mainly a teaching. We must realize that the teaching which a Christian teaches ministers something. It may minister something right, something wrong, something high, or something low. A teaching always issues in something. Based upon the issue of your teaching, your teaching may be considered as a ministry. Ministry in the biblical usage means to serve people with something, just as a waiter in a restaurant serves people with the courses of food. To serve others with something is to minister. To minister is not to preach, teach, or speak without serving anyone with anything. We may say that a certain minister who speaks for an hour ministers nothing to people. This means that according to Christ he ministered nothing, but according to the facts that minister did minister something. He ministered something wrong, something bad, or something low to people. I hope we can see that ministry produces problems, ministry produces division, and ministry produces confusion.

NOT TO TEACH DIFFERENTLY

This is why Paul wrote 1 Timothy in the midst of a confusing environment and after many years of his work with his co-workers. This Epistle is altogether an inoculation. Poison after poison was injected into the Christian church while the church was going on. At the conclusion of his writing ministry, Paul wrote 1 Timothy to inoculate the church against all these poisons. In the opening word of this Epistle, however, Paul did not write in a way that we would think to be so serious: "Even as I urged you, when I was going into Macedonia, to remain in Ephesus in order that you might charge certain ones not to teach differently" (1:3). This phrase "not to teach differently" seems so simple. If you merely read this phrase, you will not sense the seriousness of different teaching. We may not think that this is serious, but actually it is more than serious. It kills people to teach differently. To teach differently tears down God's building and annuls God's entire economy. We all must realize that even a small amount of teaching in a different way destroys the recovery. There is a proverb which says, "One sentence can build up the nation and one sentence can destroy the entire nation." You do not need to give an entire message. Just by speaking one sentence which conveys your kind of concept tears down everything. We must realize that ministry is "terrible." Your speaking can build up or destroy. It is possible that your speaking destroys, kills, and annuls.

THE UNIQUE MINISTRY

As we have seen, Paul tells Timothy in 1 Timothy 1:3 that he left him there in Ephesus to charge certain ones not to teach differently. What then, we may ask, is the unique thing which all the Christian teachers should teach? Christian teachers today teach many things such as the presbytery, baptism by immersion, the episcopalian way, holiness, how to preach the gospel, and the way to teach the Bible. We would all agree that to teach the way of Judaism is surely wrong, but what about teaching how to preach the gospel? What is wrong with preaching the gospel? We must realize that even the teaching to preach the gospel creates division. This is wrong. There is only one ministry which always builds up, edifies, and perfects with no destruction at all. There is only one unique ministry that is justified, promoted, uplifted, and even glorified in the New Testament. In 1 Timothy 1:4 Paul went on to tell Timothy what those ones who were teaching differently should be occupied with—God's economy. Through my contact with some of you brothers, I became burdened and made a quick decision to call this gathering for this training. I do not like to see the recovery destroyed by different teachings. I realize the real situation. The Lord covers me. You may not know what I am talking about because you do not know all the factors. My contact with some of you impressed me with a terrible factor. I realized that you were going to teach things differently to cause trouble and to create division. There is only one ministry that ever builds up and that never destroys—this is God's economy.

We must ask ourselves what was wrong with teaching

Judaism at the Apostle's time. This is not Buddhism or Gnosticism. To teach Judaism is to teach according to the holy Word in the Old Testament. Someone could have said to the Apostle Paul, "What is wrong with teaching the law? I am teaching the Bible." Is there anything wrong with teaching people the Bible, with teaching people theology, or with teaching people how to preach the gospel? There is nothing wrong, but we must realize that this kind of teaching creates division. In 1 Timothy Paul did not indicate that those who taught differently taught heresies or heathen things. If they had taught heathen things, no Christian would have taken them. The reason why their teachings were received is because they were scriptural things from the thirty-nine books of the Old Testament. By that time the New Testament had not yet come into existence. The holy Word was only the Old Testament. These ones who taught differently could have thought, "If you don't allow me to teach the Old Testament, then what am I going to teach? I am quite legitimate and quite scriptural." Their teaching, however, created division. Is there anything wrong with setting up a mission and sending missionaries to the field? We must realize that this is not a matter of being wrong or right, but it is a matter of "cutting Christ's Body into pieces." On the one hand, the bringing of people to Christ through the missionaries is very positive. Unconsciously, however, this kind of work cuts Christ's Body into pieces. We should be careful because we may do the same thing. We may insist, stress, and emphasize a scriptural item which seemingly is right, yet actually it cuts the Body of Christ. It divides the recovery. We must be careful. I called such a gathering because I read people's hearts from their attitude and from their spirit in speaking. I am afraid that some different teachings might be on the verge of coming out.

NOT ENOUGH TO TEACH SCRIPTURALLY

Please do not have the peace and assurance that as long as you teach things scripturally that it is alright. It is not alright because your teaching creates division. Even your right teaching creates division. We all must realize that, generally speaking, the different denominations do not teach anything wrong. They have all tried and endeavored to teach the right things, the scriptural things. Eventually, however, the Body of Christ has been cut into pieces. We thank the Lord that thousands of missionaries went to China. They brought the Bible, the gospel, and the Lord's name to China, and they brought a substantial number of God's chosen ones into the salvation of Christ. Through them, the old, conservative people of China were opened up to receive the things of the Lord. No one can deny this. On the other hand, there were some missionaries who went to China to teach different things according to their concept. As a result, they brought divisions there that have cut the Body of Christ in China into pieces and which could never be healed. What a terrible situation this is! They did something right. They preached the right thing but with a terrible issue. Who is responsible for this? The teacher who taught the right thing to create a division. This is terrible.

We should be on the alert and watchful. We do not want the right teaching. We want the teaching which teaches God's economy. Now we can understand Paul's charge in 1 Corinthians to speak the same thing (1:10). What same thing should we speak? Should we speak Bible teaching, how to meet, the way to baptize, the way to edify the saints, the way to help people to be spiritual, or the way to render much help to the Christians that they may grow in life? These are right things to teach. Something from the Bible such as evangelism is altogether right. However, if you do these things and teach them apart from God's economy, you are divisive. You are divisive in right things, in scriptural things, not in wrong things, heathen things, or pagan things. To teach the Bible and to preach the gospel are not pagan. They are altogether right and altogether scriptural, but we must be on the alert as to whether or not we are divisive. Whatever you teach should not be measured by whether it is wrong or right. It must be measured by whether it is divisive or not. Only one kind of ministry builds up and never divides—this is the unique ministry of God's economy. We must be reminded that Paul left Timothy in Ephesus with a charge to tell certain ones not to teach differently and that what they teach should be related to God's economy.

TEACHING GOD'S ECONOMY

It is impossible for anyone to control the church. No one can control the entire aggregate of Christians today. Even no one can control the Lord's recovery today. I cannot control it. Please do not think that I am controlling. I am not controlling. I cannot do it and I would not do it. To control means nothing. Paul could not control the situation in Corinth, but he charged the Lord's seekers and lovers to speak the same thing. Paul also charged his young co-worker, Timothy, to remain in the place which was under the poison of the divisive element of the right things, the scriptural things. Timothy was to charge these teachers not to teach differently. This is what we can do by following the steps of the Apostle Paul. This is what I want to do. If you mean business in the Lord's recovery, if you love the Lord, and if you are a real seeker of the Lord, you must take care of this—do not teach differently. What then should we teach? We should teach God's economy. This is the only answer available. No other result will come out of the different teachings but division. It is possible for you to do something like the missionaries, who did a great work in China, but they cut the Body of Christ into pieces. This is much more significant than what they did positively. The situation there was incurable and the Christian situation today is also incurable.

Do not consider that I am rebuking, warning, or threatening you. I am loving all of you. I am speaking a word in love because you all love the recovery. If you do love the recovery, be on the alert, not concerning others, but concerning yourself. Do not be cheated by the enemy. If you love the recovery and if you treasure the ministry, you must realize what the Lord's recovery is. The recovery is not for any kind of doing. The recovery is for God's economy in order to keep the oneness of the Body of Christ. This is the Lord's recovery. If we are through with the oneness, we are through with the recovery, and we will become another repetition of today's Christianity. Be on the alert to watch for the subtle one, the Devil, who can put any kind of mask on his face to come to you. This is my word of love. You may wonder whom I am talking about. I am talking about those of you who have an intention to teach things different than today's ministry. You know and the Lord knows whether or not you have such an intention. If you do not have such an intention, praise the Lord. That is alright. We must realize, though, that it is a serious matter to teach scriptural things and good things, yet somewhat different from God's economy.

FOUR NAMES

As we have seen in our fellowship concerning the New Testament ministry, four names in the New Testament remind us of the seriousness of getting away from God's economy. The first name is that of John the Baptist. Even he was not on the alert that he was causing trouble to make a division. He initiated the New Testament by ushering in the Savior. Eventually, however, his ministry was in danger of building up a new sect. There were two sects already among the Jews—the Pharisees and the Sadducees. The third sect would have been "the Johnites." The Lord was wise in allowing John to be in prison. The other names are Barnabas, Apollos, and even the name of the top Apostle, Peter. Even Peter was in danger of falling into division. Peter never fell into division, but his being "grey" in his ministry issued in the Corinthians taking him as a foundation of division (1 Cor. 1:12). Some in Corinth were saying that they were of Cephas, that they were of Apollos, and even that they were of Paul. Paul indicated to the Corinthians that he was nothing (1:13, 15), but Paul never said that Peter was nothing. Paul's attitude toward the Corinthians was, "Do not say you are of me. I say I am of you."

THE NEW TESTAMENT MINISTRY

The only way that can preserve us in the recovery is the unique ministry. If we say that we are in the recovery, yet we teach something so lightly, even in a concealed way, that is different from God's economy, we sow the seed that will grow up in division. Therefore, the only way that we can be preserved in the eternal oneness is to teach the same thing in God's economy. This kind of teaching is called the New Testament ministry, the ministry of the new covenant. The ministry of the new covenant is only to minister the Triune God, processed, to be dispensed into His chosen people as life and life supply to produce members of Christ to form the Body to express the Triune God. This is the New Testament economy. To teach anything, even good things and scriptural things, which is even a little bit apart from God's New Testament economy will still issue in division and that will be very much used by the subtle one, the evil one. We must, therefore, be on the alert.

CHAPTER FIVE

THE NEED TO BE CONSTITUTED AND THE GOVERNING PRINCIPLE OF THE DIVINE DISPENSING IN GOD'S DISPENSATIONS

THE NEED TO BE CONSTITUTED

In the earlier chapters, we have seen what the New Testament ministry is and what the vision in the Lord's recovery is. This is why we must see how to carry out the vision. To carry out the vision, we need to be constituted with the New Testament ministry. The New Testament ministry must be our constitution. As long as you can teach something different from the New Testament ministry, this indicates that you have never been constituted with it. From my youth as a Chinese child I have been constituted with the Chinese language. In one meeting I intended to speak English, but unintentionally Chinese words came out of my mouth. This is because I have merely learned English, but Chinese is my constitution. Whatever you have been constituted with will come out sooner or later. The Lord's recovery has never been constituted into your being. If it were, you could never teach anything different. This is just like a person's native language being constituted into his being. What he is constituted with, he speaks. This is why I am burdened. We need to see where we are and what the Lord really wants us to be in His recovery.

Since the first century, many of God's chosen people came into the New Testament ministry and many left. Who would have ever thought that Barnabas would leave? He was wonderful and he was the one who brought in Saul of Tarsus to be a great apostle (Acts 9:27; 11:25-26). Barnabas initiated Saul and then he left (Acts 15:38-39). Peter was also in danger of leaving the New Testament ministry. Even before Peter shrunk back from eating with Gentile believers out of fear of those of the circumcision (Gal. 2:11-14), he was on the border of the New Testament ministry in Acts 10. Through his three and a half years with the Lord during His earthly ministry and through Pentecost Peter got into the New Testament ministry in full. He was the central figure of the New Testament ministry in Acts 2—5, but in Acts 10 he was on the border, even "on the fringe of the roof." He was on the verge of falling away from the New Testament ministry. The Lord was merciful because He had to use Peter. The Lord came to him in the Old Testament way of a vision to move him from the "fringe of the roof" of the New Testament to the center. Thus, he was preserved.

We also have seen that there was a problem with James in Jerusalem and that Peter was influenced. Galatians 2 shows us that Peter had fallen away from the truth of the New Testament ministry, so Paul rebuked him. This is because the New Testament ministry was not that thoroughly instituted into Peter as it was into Paul. Paul received a kind of constitution so that his entire being was for the New Testament ministry. We may not preach differently, but some of us may have a little doubt about the recovery. Even that little doubt is an indication that the institution of the New Testament economy into you may not be that thorough. In other words, you may still not be thoroughly constituted with God's New Testament ministry.

I saw much opposition to the Lord's recovery for twenty years in mainland China. Later, I was sent out from Taiwan to southeast Asia and then to the United States. I personally have confronted opposition even from saints among us. Over the years, though, I must testify that I have never had a bit of doubt about the Lord's recovery. Before I came out of mainland China, the New Testament ministry had been thoroughly constituted into my being. I know many doctrines, but I cannot teach those doctrines. My person has become a constitution of the New Testament ministry. Whenever you ask me to speak and wherever you ask me to speak, whether it is at a wedding, at your dining table, to your family, to the old, to the young, to the brothers, or to the sisters, what I can speak and what I will speak is the New Testament ministry. How do we carry out this ministry? We need to be a person constituted with God's New Testament ministry. If you mean business with the Lord and if you love the Lord for His recovery and you love His recovery for the Lord you must get yourself constituted with this New Testament ministry.

Our constitution should not be something gilded. It must be something inwrought into our being. The Great Babylon is gilded with gold (Rev. 17:4), but the lampstand is golden by its intrinsic essence. It is golden intrinsically, basically, and essentially. With many of us, our being golden is somewhat by gilding. Something that is gilded with gold cannot pass the test of "scratching." A little scratch exposes the real nature of the thing. If we are really gold, "scratching" will expose that we are gold. Even if someone were to "break us up" and "grind us into powder," it would show that we are not only golden but gold. If our intrinsic nature is golden, this can stand any kind of test. The Lord's recovery does not treasure any gilded thing. We treasure the basic things, the intrinsic things, the essential things.

Please do not think that I am encouraging you or charging you to learn the Life-studies. The Lord Jesus indicates in John 6 that His Word is the bread of life (vv. 48, 63). To receive bread is not to learn about it but to eat it. To eat something means to receive it into your organic body. The food that you have received into your stomach becomes your blood, cells, fiber, and tissue. It becomes you. Merely to learn the messages does not mean much. We must take in the Word and let the Word be organically assimilated into our entire being. Then when you speak and when you give messages in the principle of the teachings conveyed in the Life-study messages, you will not merely speak from the printed page. You will speak out of your "fiber." Then your speaking will stir up much interest and the impact will be there. This is not eloquence. Eloquence means nothing. You must become constituted with the New Testament ministry.

THE LIFE-STUDY MESSAGES

Some condemn us and slander us by saying that we take the Life-study messages more than the Bible and even as the Bible because we use them so much. We must ask, though, which students of the Bible and which teachers of the Bible have never used commentaries, expositions, or other books. Commentaries and expositions are not for the purpose of replacing the Bible but for the purpose of opening up the Bible, which is somewhat hard for us to enter in. Because we need the help of reference books, this does not mean that we replace the Bible with reference books. Those of us who have read the Life-study messages can testify that these Life-studies with the Recovery Version and all the footnotes open the Bible to us whenever we touch them. The Life-studies and the Recovery Version not only convey the nourishment to us, but they become an opener.

After reading some of the Life-study messages on Romans 8, for example, I think we can testify that Romans has been opened to us. For years I have been a very devoted seeker of biblical truth. Romans 8 was seemingly opened to me before 1954, but I did not realize that it was still concealed to me. I did not see that Romans 8 actually is a revelation of the processed Triune God dispensing Himself into the tripartite man. Without such an unveiling you cannot enter into Romans 8. We must see that the processed Triune God is dispensing Himself into His redeemed, tripartite man, making this man a man of life—first his spirit is life (v. 10), then his mind becomes life (v. 6), and finally, life is given to his mortal body (v. 11). Until you have seen such a vision you could never enter into Romans 8. Without such a vision, Romans 8 is concealed and closed to you. Once you have received such a vision, however, you will receive not only nourishment but enlightenment. You receive the key that opens Romans 8. This is not replacing the Bible. This is not replacing Romans 8 with the Life-study messages, but this is to get the help from the Life-study messages to enter into Romans 8.

Many commentaries and expositions have been written on the book of Romans. Not one, however, according to my knowledge, has ever pointed out that Romans is composed of four sections—from justification to sanctification to the Body of Christ and finally to the local churches. No other commentary said that the book of Romans ends with the local churches. This, however, is the fact. If you read the book of Romans by yourself without any help, I am afraid that you will not see that this book ends with the local churches and that the revelation in this book intends to bring you from a sinner to a son of God and a member of Christ to the local churches. We need this vision today. We can understand such a vision with the help of some proper, advanced exposition like the notes of the Recovery Version and the Life-study messages. If the Recovery Version, the notes, the outlines, the cross-references, and the messages were Brother Nee's writings, I would spend day after day to go out and promote them. Because they are my writings, I am restricted in what I would say. To a certain extent, however, I have become "a fool" to promote my own writings (2 Cor. 11:1; 12:11). I have received many letters of appreciation from the saints thanking me for the help they have received. Recently, one sister said that she wanted to write and tell me how much the Life-studies have helped her. She said that she received the help from reading the Life-studies when she was in a desperate situation. She had no way out, but when she read the Life-studies she received the help.

THE NEED OF REGULATING RULES AND PRINCIPLES

We need to get into all these precious gifts which the Lord has been giving us in the past sixty years. To get into these things we must practice what was fellowshipped in the last two chapters. All of you should be encouraged not to be contented with what you already know, but you need to go further to develop more and more. We should all be those driving forward and not backward. To drive forward, however, we need regulations. We are restricted as to where we can drive by the highway itself. Also, on the highway are white lines which indicate to us that we need to be restricted in our driving on the highway. Otherwise, you will kill yourself. I have opened the door for you all to "sail on" and develop. Without restriction, however, you will drive yourself into "the

Pacific Ocean." It is possible that your driving could kill others, but you yourself could be saved. You may say that you are okay, but others were killed. Morally speaking, you are held responsible. In like manner, in our development of the truth, we must develop the truth based upon what we have seen. What we have seen is a foundation and "the shoulders" for us to stand on. To go further in developing the truth you must have some regulating rules and principles.

When I lived in Shanghai, there was a Seventh-Day Adventist denomination there. They once published a big paper with a lot of prophecies. One of these prophecies said that America was one of the ten kingdoms of the coming Roman empire. This is an example of expounding the Bible without regulations. The traffic on the earth must be regulated, and even the air traffic has its regulations; otherwise, many lives would be lost. In like manner, to interpret typology, prophecy, or any portion of the Bible there are basic rules and principles to follow.

Interpreting the Good Land

Some have interpreted the land of Canaan, the good land, as a type of heaven and the Jordan River as a type of death. Many hymnals mention the Jordan River. I still remember a hymn which referred to the cold wave in the Jordan River which we had to pass through to get to heaven, the good land. When I was a young man I received this interpretation with no peace. I received it because everyone believed it was true and I thought it was probably right. It seemed alright to say that after death we go to heaven, so the good land of Canaan must be a type of heaven. Later, however, I was told that if the land of Canaan were a type of heaven that would mean that heaven would be a terrible place, full of Canaanites, Hittites, Amorites, Perizzites, Hivites, and Jebusites, full of enemies (Exo. 3:8), and full of giants (Num. 13:32-33). In our hymnal we have 1080 hymns. Approximately two hundred of these hymns were written by us and the others were selected from other sources. A number of these hymns ended with the thought of crossing the river to enter heaven. This was very popular in the last century. This is why we changed the endings of these hymns. Because the statute of limitation on these hymns was over and they were in the public domain, we had the liberty to change them so that they would be according to the truth.

Another interpretation of the significance of the good land of Canaan came from the inner-life writings. They said that Canaan was not a type of heaven because there is no war in heaven. Therefore, there are no Canaanites in heaven. They said that Canaan typified the battlefield in the spiritual warfare where the overcoming saints fight the battle. Temporarily, I felt that this was right, but eventually I discovered that this interpretation does not fit with the children of Israel being a type of God's people in God's economy.

When I came to Taiwan in 1949, I was clear after much consideration that Canaan was not a type of heaven. I was also somewhat clear that Canaan could not be a type of the battlefield of the spiritual warfare. I was seeking very honestly to know what the significance of the good land of Canaan was in typology. I believe that eventually the Lord showed me, especially in the year 1959. It was then that I had a thorough study with the saints in Taiwan on the Pentateuch. At that time I was made clear that Canaan was a type of the all-inclusive Christ for God's people's enjoyment. This interpretation is based upon the history of the children of Israel. They were slaves in Egypt who were redeemed. God's judgment passed over them and they enjoyed the Savior as the nourishing and redeeming Lamb. The Lamb was their enjoyment. By eating the Lamb, which was the beginning of their redeemed life, they were energized to cross the Red Sea to journey to God's destination. On the way in the wilderness they received the manna every day as a further nourishment. From the wilderness they entered into the good land, and Joshua tells us that after they entered into the good land the manna ceased and they began to enjoy the produce of the good land (Josh. 5:12). Therefore, the good land must typify the rich, all-inclusive enjoyment of Christ to God's people.

From 1959 I began to minister boldly that Canaan was a type of Christ in an all-inclusive way for God's people's enjoyment. After I came to the United States in 1962, I gave a series of messages in the first conference in the United States on the all-inclusive Christ, based upon Deuteronomy 8:7-10. These messages were a great opener, which not only opened others' eyes but also opened my eyes. This is why I tell you not to follow the expositions, commentaries, and interpretations in a blind way. You need to pick up some principles to govern the interpretation of the types in the Old Testament, such as the historical events and geographical places. The basic principle is Christ being the enjoyment of God's people. Egypt typified a land of slavery. There was no enjoyment for God's people until the redemption of God came in. Then God's redeemed people began to enjoy, not merely God's blessing, but the very Redeemer who is Jehovah, the Lord Jesus Christ, to be their enjoyment. At the beginning of their journey they enjoyed Christ, not only as the redeeming Lamb, but also as the nourishing Lamb. Then they took their journey and on the way they enjoyed Christ again as the heavenly manna in the wilderness, as their daily portion. When they entered into the good land, they immediately enjoyed the produce of the good land. Here is a principle which governs our interpretation of all the historical events and of all the geographical places in the type of the children of Israel.

The Recovery of Doctrines

From the Reformation to the present time many different "truths" have been recovered in the Lord's recovery. Actually their recoveries were not recoveries of truth, but of doctrine. The presbytery is not a truth but a doctrine. Baptism by immersion is not a truth but a doctrine. In the seventeenth century in northern Europe certain ones began to see that all Christians are brothers. Eventually in the eighteenth century the Moravian brothers under the leadership of Zinzendorf began to practice the church life as brothers. Even the brotherhood, though, is not a truth but a doctrine. Even the teaching concerning holiness and sanctification is not a truth but a doctrine. This doctrine talks about outward things. To be sanctified is to be sinless and not to be worldly. As I have mentioned already, all of these doctrines became different teachings, different ministries, which issued in sects.

Schools of Theology

From the Reformation to the present time different theologies have been taught. Today there is the Catholic theology, and with the Protestants is reformed theology. Another theology may be termed dispensational theology. According to reformed theology, the Old Testament and the New Testament are the same with no difference. This is like making a person's face flat with no distinctions for the eyes, nose, mouth, or ears. The teaching of reformed theology is wrong. Another kind of theology is what I call secular theology which is taught in the secular universities as a department for the learning of human culture. In human culture there is a section of religion, including a section of Christian religion. People study this kind of theology in a secular way. At some of these secular universities, the students learn theology just like people learn art in the school of art. We should not follow either the reformed theology or the secular theology.

Dispensations

The word dispensation, biblically speaking, was rightly understood by the school of dispensational theology. They say that God has different ways of dealing with man from Adam to the end of the millennium. Scofield took the lead to say that in God's dealing with the human race He has seven arrangements. He said this because this word dispensation is a translation of the Greek word *oikonomia* which means a kind of household management, arrangement or administration. The dispensational theologians understood this word rightly in saying that in God's dealing with the human race there are seven arrangements from Adam to the end of the millennium. These dispensations are the dispensations of innocence, conscience, human government, promise, law, grace, and the kingdom. Some of the stricter Brethren teachers, though, say that according to Romans 5:14 there should be just four main dispensations. This verse has in it the phrase "from Adam until Moses." The dispensation before law is, as Romans 5:14 says, from Adam to Moses. The dispensation of law is from Moses to Christ's first coming. Then the dispensation of grace is from His first coming to His second coming. Finally, the fourth dispensation is the dispensation of the kingdom. This is more scriptural. The word dispensation was rightly understood by these Brethren teachers, but their understanding of the significance of God's dispensation was very short. They only saw that the dispensations were God's arrangements for Him to carry out His purpose. They did not see that God's dispensation, God's arrangement, or the arrangement of His divine administration, has a purpose. His purpose is to dispense Himself into His chosen and redeemed people. This purpose has been nearly fully missed by the dispensational theologians, and they are the good theologians.

The Central View of the Divine Dispensation

The shortcoming of the dispensational teachings has never been pointed out as it is today. We have the boldness and the light to say this because through the past forty years the Lord has shown us the New Testament economy plus the New Testament ministry. Based upon this, we have the light, the boldness, and the assurance to say that the dispensational teachings are right but missing the goal. God did have four main dispensations, but these dispensations are for one unique purpose—to dispense Himself into His chosen people as everything. This is why I had the burden in May of 1983 in Stuttgart to minister on this one thing—to show that the dispensations have a purpose, a goal, and a central view to dispense God Himself into His chosen people. These messages have been published with a title "The Central View of the Divine Dispensation." I hope that you would spend some time to read these messages again by picking up the crucial points. If you read them again in the way that I presented to you in the previous two chapters you will see something crucial. You will see that God's dispensations are for His dispensing. Dispensation means household arrangement, but dispensing means to pass out, to distribute, the processed Triune God as life and as life supply to be our spiritual, heavenly, and divine supply.

In the Old Testament, Joseph distributed the rich food of

Pharaoh to the hungry, famished ones. As a New Testament Joseph, Paul took the lead to do this and we are his followers to pass out the Triune God, processed, as the very divine food to feed all the hungry people of the earth. This is the governing principle. I was strongly taught by the Brethren that to interpret the entire Bible you need to take care of the dispensations. Merely to take care of the dispensations, however, is not adequate. You must take care of the dispensing of the dispensations. This must be and is the basic, great principle to govern our interpretation of the Bible. When you young brothers, standing on our shoulders, go on to develop the truth, you must be ruled by this principle—the principle of the divine dispensing in God's dispensations.

Chapter Six

THE GOVERNING PRINCIPLES
OF CHRIST AND THE CHURCH
AND OF CHRIST, THE SPIRIT, LIFE,
AND THE CHURCH

CHRIST AND THE CHURCH

We have seen that to develop ourselves in the truth we need basic principles to rule us and to govern us. Now we must see that there is a further governing principle which is very basic—Christ and the church. Your developing of any truth must be based upon Christ and the church. This should be and must be your governing principle. Do not pick up aspects from the Bible not related to Christ and the church.

For example, Ephesians 5 tells us that wives should be subject to their own husbands (v. 22) and that husbands should love their wives (v. 25). From my youth I heard the pastors and Christian teachers teach these things. These things, however, should not be separated from Christ and the church (v. 32). The woman's submission and the man's love are taught in the Bible with Christ for the church. Without Christ, who can submit or who can love? Fallen mankind's nature is rebellious and hateful. There is no submission or love within fallen mankind. There is nothing but rebellion and hatred. Without Christ, who can love or who can submit? Therefore, the Bible teaches us women's submission and men's love with Christ. We must be filled in spirit with Christ (Eph. 5:18). Then love comes out and submission comes out. If we develop submission and love without Christ this is wrong. This becomes Confucius's ethics. A biblical submission is not only with Christ, but also for the church.

After over twenty years experience of the church life in the

United States, we have seen that whoever loves the church has the best family life. Whoever is for the church has the best marriage life, but the family life and the marriage life of those who have left the church goes downhill. By the Lord's mercy, the rate of separation and divorce is lowest in the local church. You must love Christ and love the church. If you do, as a wife you will submit and as a husband you will love. This again is the way to develop the truth based upon and governed by the principle of Christ and the church.

Holiness, humility, kindness, victory, and spirituality must be developed with Christ for the church. To allegorize any kind of case in the Bible, both in the Old and New Testaments, you must allegorize with Christ and for the church. Then you are safe, and whatever you say is right because the entire Bible was written according to the basic principle—with Christ for the church. Even the great Babylon on the negative side must be understood in the light of Christ and the church. The safeguarding key of the ministry is "with Christ for the church." I have allegorized many portions of the Word and have put out many publications by this key and governing principle. We have even published a book on the Psalms under the view of this governing principle. The title of this book is *Christ and the Church Revealed and Typified in the Psalms*. The principle of "with Christ for the church" safeguards you, rules you, supports you, and enriches you. An interpretation of the Psalms using this key will be filled with the divine riches.

In our developing in the truth we must first keep the principle of the Triune God dispensing Himself into His chosen people. This is one of the basic principles that governs our interpreting of the Bible. The second basic principle is Christ and the church. In the past, the Brethren told people that to interpret the Bible you must be dispensational. As a young man under the feet of the great teachers among the Brethren assemblies, I was charged definitely and repeatedly not to interpret the New Testament according to the Old Testament since they are in two dispensations. The understanding of dispensations helps to some extent, but this is too shallow. To interpret the Bible according to the principle of the Triune

God dispensing Himself into His chosen people is much deeper, higher, and more profound. Another deeper principle is that we must interpret the Bible "with Christ for the church."

Even the first two chapters of Genesis should be interpreted under this governing principle. In Genesis 1:26 we see Christ as the image of God. God created man in His own image in Genesis, and in the New Testament Colossians 1:15 tells us that God's image is Christ. In Genesis 2:9 we see the tree of life, which also refers to Christ. Adam is also a type of Christ being the Head of all God's creation. God's image outwardly, God's life inwardly, and the Head of all creation is Christ. If we develop these items with Christ we are on the right way. With Adam's wife Eve we see the church (Gen. 2:21-25). The first two chapters of the Bible show us Christ with the church.

We must realize that these first two chapters govern the entire Bible. After these two chapters man fell, and that began another story. This is why we can see that the consummation of the Bible in Revelation 21 and 22 corresponds with the first two chapters of the Bible. These four chapters correspond with each other, and both are with Christ for the church. This is the principle for the beginning of the Bible and for the consummation of the Bible. Also, the entire Bible between these four chapters must also be interpreted with Christ for the church. Even though so many negative things came in, they are related indirectly to Christ and indirectly to the church by providing a black background to help our understanding. Now we can see that we can interpret the entire Bible with Christ for the church.

CHRIST, THE SPIRIT, LIFE, AND THE CHURCH

Another principle which we must take in our interpretation of the Bible is the principle of four items: Christ, the Spirit, life, and the church. The first principle we have seen is a general principle—the Triune God dispensing Himself into His chosen people. The second principle is in more detail—with Christ for the church. Now we see a third principle of Christ, the Spirit, life, and the church. Any message or any development of the Bible without Christ, the Spirit, life, and the church is an empty shell with no content. The content of the Bible is Christ, the Spirit, life, and the church. At least one of these items must be present in your development of the truth. Also, in your preaching of the gospel at least one of these items should be present. I saw some evangelists in China who preached quite prevailingly, but in their gospel they did not preach much reality of Christ, the Spirit, life, and the church. Their prevailing evangelical work attracted a good number of people. However, many of these people turned to the way of the Lord's recovery to pick up Christ, the Spirit, life, and the church. They all remained and became very useful to the Lord's interest. Those who did not turn this way, including the evangelists, either disappeared or still remained with emptiness. In their gospel campaigns a number were saved, but after ten years many disappeared or remained empty. We must thank the Lord, however, that many also turned this way. The ones who turned this way not only remained but they became solid with the truth concerning Christ, the Spirit, life, and the church.

D. L. Moody's preaching, comparatively speaking, was more solid than any other evangelist in England. If you compare Moody's messages to the other evangelists' messages of his day, you can see that with Moody's messages there is some solid content, while with the others you can see mostly eloquence. Some evangelists preach with eloquent illustrations to attract people to stir up their interest, but after being interested, all that is left with them is a good story. Many are merely eloquent speakers with very little Christ. Based upon this principle, we should check today's preaching. How much Christ, the Spirit, life, and the church is in today's preaching of the Word? This shows us the emptiness of today's preaching and teaching. You should not develop the truth in the Bible in this way, in an empty way. You must develop the biblical truth in the way of Christ, the Spirit, life, and the church. Even if you have a good portion of the Word with a good idea to stir up people's interest, you must consider whether or not Christ, the Spirit, life, and the church are the content of your message. If they are not the content, you should forget about it. Do not go further to develop anything apart from this governing principle because you will waste your time. Also, you will have no safeguard and you will be led astray.

All the heresies came in by the way of developing the truth in the Bible apart from Christ, the Spirit, life, and the church. Any doctrine developed apart from these four items will issue in heresy or division. The Presbyterian church came into existence because they developed the doctrine of presbytery without Christ, without the Spirit, without life, and without the church. If they had developed the truth of the presbytery with the church, they would have dared not set up a Presbyterian church. The Presbyterian church became one among many divisions. Some even developed the doctrine of holiness apart from Christ, the Spirit, life, and the church. We, however, should develop the doctrine of holiness with Christ for the church. We need to tell people that holiness is Christ Himself, and this Christ today is the life-giving Spirit (1 Cor. 15:45). Not only is His Spirit called the Holy Spirit, but also He is called the life-giving Spirit who imparts the divine life into us for our sanctification. Holiness is God's nature and is related to life. If you do not have God's life, you do not have God's nature, which is holiness. If God's holiness is going to be increased within you, you must live according to God's nature and by God's life. We must also realize that this holy life should not only be for our personal living but it must also be a part of the church life. If we would develop the doctrine of holiness with Christ, with the Spirit, with life, and with the church, we would see a marvelous revelation. Otherwise, a holiness sect will be created. This is why some have established holiness churches. These are actually holiness divisions cutting the Body into pieces.

It is dangerous to develop any biblical doctrine apart from Christ, the Spirit, life, and the church. To do this could lead to division. Your doctrine, on the other hand, may not be wrong, but eventually the issue of your practice will be a division. It is always safe to develop any doctrine in the Bible with Christ, the Spirit, life, and the church. Even if something is good and scriptural, never develop it apart from Christ, the Spirit, life, and the church. While the principle of dispensations helps in interpreting the Bible, it is too superficial. Always remember these three intrinsic principles of developing the truth in the Bible: the Triune God dispensing Himself into His chosen and redeemed people; Christ and the church; and Christ, the Spirit, life, and the church.

CHAPTER SEVEN

THE DIVINE TRINITY

(1)

THE ESSENTIAL TRINITY
AND THE ECONOMICAL TRINITY

Thus far, the two main aspects we have seen concerning the divine Trinity are the essential Trinity and the economical Trinity. In the essential Trinity, the Father, the Son, and the Spirit coexist and coinhere at the same time and in the same way with no succession. There is no first, second, or third. However, in God's plan, in God's administrative arrangement, in God's economy, the Father takes the first step, the Son takes the second step, and the Spirit takes the third step. The Father planned, the Son accomplished, and the Spirit applies what the Son accomplished according to the Father's plan. This is a successive procedure or a succession in God's economy to carry out His eternal purpose. The essential Trinity refers to the essence of the Triune God for His existence; the economical Trinity refers to His plan for His move. There is the need of the existence of the divine Trinity, and there is also the need of the plan of the divine Trinity.

Modalism

Modalism teaches that the Father, the Son, and the Spirit are not all eternal and do not all exist at the same time, but are merely three temporary consecutive manifestations of the one God. Modalism says that the Father was there and then when the Son came the Father was over. Furthermore, when the Spirit came, the Son was over. Modalists say that the three are one, but their interpretation jeopardizes the existence of the Trinity. They do not have a clear view concerning the difference between the essence and the economy of the Trinity. In essence, the three of the Godhead exist equally at the same time and coinhere equally at the same time from eternity to eternity.

The Father's Plan, the Son's Accomplishment, and the Spirit's Application

In addition, God, the Triune God, has a purpose, so He made a plan. He made an administrative arrangement to carry out His purpose, so He has an economy. In this economy the three of the Godhead are in succession. This is economical, not essential. Furthermore, to carry out the plan there is the need of much work. The Father accomplished the first step of the plan, of the economy. He worked in choosing us and in predestinating us. The work of selection and the work of predestination were done by the Father, not by the Son or by the Spirit. We must be careful, though, to realize that the Father did the selection and the predestination, but He did not do them alone. The Father of the Triune Godhead did the choosing and the predestinating in the Son and with the Spirit. If we say that the Father chose us and selected us alone, we jeopardize the coinherence and the coexistence of the divine Trinity. The coinherence and the coexistence of the Triune God are from eternity to eternity.

After the plan was made, there was the need for the Son to come to carry out the plan. The Son came to be incarnated, to be flesh, to be a man. He came to live a human life for thirty-three and a half years, to die an all-inclusive death, and to resurrect from the dead. The Son came to do all the works, but He did not do these works alone. He did them with the Father and by the Spirit. The Son came to do His all-inclusive redemptive work, which includes incarnation, human living, death, and resurrection, with the Father and by the Spirit. If the Son had come by Himself alone, this again would have jeopardized the coexistence and the coinherence, the essence, of the divine Trinity.

After the accomplishment there was the need and there still is the need of application. In this third step of application more fine works are needed. In the first step the Father had only to make a plan. In the second step, the Son had to accomplish the plan with much work. The Spirit's application in the third step needs a great deal of continuous work. We need the Spirit to lead us and to guide us not only day by day but also minute by minute in all the details of our daily life. The Spirit needs to be applied in your talk to your wife and even in your attitude. We can see how fine and how detailed is the work to carry out this application. The Spirit is doing this application work not alone by Himself, but as the Son with the Father. Otherwise, this application would also jeopardize the divine existence of the Trinity.

In the work of the Father's plan we can say that the Father did the works in the Son and with the Spirit, but we cannot say that the Son did that work with the Father and by the Spirit. Neither can we say that the Spirit did the works of the plan as the Son, with the Father. Also, in the second step of God's economy, the step of accomplishment, the Son did all the works. We cannot say the Father did the accomplishing work with the Son and by the Spirit. Neither can we say that the Spirit accomplished the Father's plan as the Son, with the Father. We can only say that the Son did all the works to accomplish the Father's plan with the Father and by the Spirit. Also, we cannot say that the Father became flesh and that the Father lived on this earth in the flesh. Furthermore, we cannot say that the Father went to the cross and died for our redemption, and we cannot say the blood shed on the cross is the blood of Jesus the Father. We must say that the blood was shed by Jesus the Son of God (1 John 1:7). We can neither say that the Father died on the cross nor can we say that the Father resurrected from the dead.

In the third step of God's economy, the step of the Spirit, all the works were surely done by the Spirit. In the third step, however, the Son became the Spirit. Therefore, whatever kind of work is done by the Spirit is the work done by the Son as the Spirit. In the third step, all the works are done by the Spirit as the Son with the Father. We cannot say, though, that all the works in the third step are done by the Father with the Son and through the Spirit. We need a sober mind to see this.

In the third step all the works are done by the Spirit as the Son with the Father. We can also say that all the works in the third step are done by the Son as the Spirit with the Father because after the second step was accomplished, the Son as the Accomplisher, with the Father, became the Spirit. Therefore, the Spirit is the ultimate consummation of the processed Triune God in His economy. Every work that is done by the Spirit is done by the Son as the Spirit with the Father.

THE TRIUNE GOD AND THE DIVINE TRINITY

Now we need to go on to see the difference between the Triune God and the divine Trinity. The Triune God mainly refers to God Himself, and the divine Trinity mainly refers to God's being Triune, which is the main attribute of the Godhead. It is more correct to refer the divine dispensing to the divine Trinity rather than to the Triune God. The Triune God refers to God the Person, while the divine Trinity refers to the main attribute of the Godhead. For example, saying that someone is a faithful person is different from saying that he is faithfulness. A faithful person refers to the man. His faithfulness refers to his being faithful, his virtue. In a general way God is dispensing Himself into us, but in a particular, actual, and practical way God is dispensing His Trinity into us.

The New Testament reveals that the Father is in us, the Son is in us, the Spirit is in us, and God is in us. Ephesians 4:6 shows us that the Father is in us: "One God and Father of all, who is over all and through all and in all." John 14:23 also shows us that the Father is in the believer: "If anyone loves Me, he will keep My word, and My Father will love him, and We will come to him and make an abode with him." Second Corinthians 13:5 is one verse which reveals that the Son is in us. Romans 8:9 shows us that the Spirit dwells in us. The strongest verse showing us that God is in us is Philippians 2:13: "For it is God who operates in you both the willing and the working for His good pleasure." We should never forget Philippians 2:13. God is not only in us, but He is also operating or working in us. God is in us as the Triune God, the Father, the Son, and the Spirit. The Triune God being in us, however, may be merely terminology to us. We may not have the practical experience of the Trinity of the Godhead. We are not only experiencing God but also experiencing the Trinity of the Godhead. The Father is in us, the Son is in us, and the Spirit is in us. These are not three persons, but these are the Trinity of the one God. In other words, this divine Trinity is the strongest attribute of the Godhead. His faithfulness, His love, His kindness, and other attributes are not above this attribute. The top attribute of the divine Person is His Trinity. His Trinity is constituted solely with His Person, and His Person is in the Trinity—the Father, the Son, and the Spirit.

This is why the ancient theologians used a word to describe the very substance of the Trinity—hypostasis. This word comes from Greek, *hupo* meaning under and *stasis* meaning something substantial supporting from beneath. Hypostasis is singular and hypostases is plural. This anglicized Greek word means the supporting or substantial essence from beneath, and refers to the constitution of the Triune Godhead being the Father, the Son, and the Spirit. In theology the denotation of the word hypostases was gradually changed to persons. This is why one of the meanings for hypostasis in Webster's dictionary is person. This is a theological definition. We must see, however, that the divine Trinity is the constitution of the Triune God. The divine dispensing of the divine Trinity means to dispense the constitution of our Triune God into our being to make His constitution ours.

A WORD OF LOVE

Because some brothers' understanding of the things concerning the Lord and His interest was too superficial, I nearly had no way to help them. In 1967 in Elden hall there was a lot of talk about the way to practice the church life. I stood up to tell the saints that I had been practicing the church life for years and years and that I knew what I was doing here. I said, "I don't like to argue with you. If you feel your way is right, go to do it. Don't make the church in Los Angeles a lab for you. We don't need a lab here in Los Angeles. I have practiced the church life for many years and have established many churches. In every church, I had a success. I have the full assurance that what we are doing is right and proper. We don't need a lab. If you want to do lab work, go to another place to practice your lab. If you will be successful, come back to me and I will be the first one to follow you. But I assure you that if you go, you will have a failure. This is my word of love. It is up to you whether you take it or not." That talk to the church stopped all the "different talks."

I must testify that I am not afraid of today's opposition. If some person says that 2×2 is 4 no one can defeat him. Even if another person says that 2×2 is 3.9999999, he still is not right. What I have been teaching to you I have studied thoroughly for over fifty years, not only according to the pure Word of God but also by checking with my own and others' experiences. You do not know how much time I have spent day and night to study. Through our fellowship in this training I want to assure you that there is no need to be doubtful concerning what you have received through this ministry concerning the Lord's recovery today. You should not be affected by others. If you take this way, you will be blessed. If you do not take this way, you will miss the blessing. This is up to you. If you feel you are right, go ahead and take another way. The years will test your way. You will come back either to repent or you will remain in that failure. Through the years we have seen some who have left and who are still remaining in their failure. It is a sad thing. I love them, but just cannot help them. Some of the opposers take my words and say that I threaten people. I say strongly that I do not threaten people and that I never threaten people. I love people. For example, the proper gospel preaching is always a word of love. If someone preaching the gospel says, "If you do not repent, you will go to hell," is this a kind of threatening? This is not a threat, but a loving word to help the sinners to turn from their wrong way.

We must realize that the recovery today is in 1984. In 1922 the recovery was in an experimental stage, but today it is no longer that much an experimental operation. The work in the United States is my "fifth factory." The past four factories were all successful, so I have the full assurance that this is the way. I sent out an urgent notice to call such an urgent gathering to present to you the New Testament ministry, the vision of the Lord's recovery, and the way to carry out the vision. This is my word of love. If you like to consider this as threatening, it is up to you. I do not like to pretend. I do not like to be so mild outwardly, yet inwardly another way. I am what I am inwardly. I have no intention of threatening you or of warning you. I say this out of my love. I love you brothers, and even more I love the Lord's recovery. I have sacrificed my entire life with my future for this. I would not like to see the recovery "cut into pieces" and damaged.

CHAPTER EIGHT

THE DIVINE TRINITY

(2)

In the history of theological study concerning the divine Trinity, three words have been used—essence, hypostasis, and substance. We need to clarify the meaning of these three words, which we have already mentioned in relation to the divine Trinity.

ESSENCE

We can see what the word essence means in the study of the divine Trinity by defining two related words—element and nature. An element is a substance. In the New Jerusalem there are three elements—gold, pearls, and precious stones. Therefore, in the building of the New Jerusalem there are three substances or elements. Every element has its nature and in the nature of the element is the essence. Consequently, the essence denotes the very thing itself. Now we can see that there is a difference in using the two words essence and substance. We cannot refer to the substance of the essence but to the essence of the substance. Each substance or substantial element has its essence.

It is clearly revealed in the Bible that God is an eternal God. The eternal God has His existence and with His existence there must be the essence. Without essence there is not existence. Anything that exists has an essence, so essence actually refers mostly to God's existence. Our God is the eternal God existing from eternity to eternity. His existence tells us that He has the essence which we call the divine essence.

HYPOSTASIS

Another word used in relation to the Trinity is hypostasis. This anglicized Greek word is actually composed of two Greek words—*hupo* meaning under or below and *stasis* meaning substantial support. The word, therefore, means the substantial support underneath. This is like the four legs of a table being the substantial support underneath. Hypostasis in English simply means substantial support. The Father, the Son, and the Spirit are the three hypostases or substances of the divine Trinity or of the Godhead.

Gradually, however, this word has been used in the sense of person. This understanding is far off and causes trouble. To say that the Father, the Son, and the Spirit are three hypostases is correct, but to say definitely that the Father, the Son, and the Spirit are three persons is going a little too far. Griffith Thomas indicated that we may borrow a word like person to define the Trinity because our human language is inadequate, but if we press the term person too far, it will lead to tritheism. Even to use the word hypostasis is not completely safe because when we use any terms, vocabulary, or illustrations to define the divine Trinity, we always run a risk. The divine Trinity is too much of a mystery. Our finite mentality is incapable of understanding the divine Trinity in full. We do not have the adequate vocabulary to describe Him because in our human culture there is not such a mysterious thing as the divine Trinity. Because there is not such a thing, we do not have the vocabulary, and even in our mentality we do not have the logic to understand the divine Trinity.

SUBSTANCE

In the historical study of the divine Trinity, the word hypostasis was first used and then the word substance. Hypostasis and substance are synonyms in theological study. Then the word essence was picked up. In the substance there is the essence. In the study of the divine Trinity the following crucial statement was made—the Triune God has three substances but only one essence. This statement is more safe. The Triune God is essentially one but substantially three. The Triune God is one in His essence, but He is three in His substance. To say that God has three essences is wrong, but to say that God has three substances is correct. Three substances equals three hypostases and, as some say, three hypostases equals three persons. Therefore, substantially speaking God is three, and essentially speaking God is one. This is the essential Trinity. In essence, the Father, the Son, and the Spirit are one, but in substance (person) They are three. Actually, we do not appreciate the word persons that much. Rather, we appreciate the word hypostases. I hope this fellowship has provided "a simple map" of the understanding of the words element, nature, essence, substance, hypostasis, and person.

GOD'S ECONOMY

Also, God is very purposeful. Ephesians 1 reveals that God has His good pleasure, His heart's desire (vv. 5, 9). God made a purpose according to His good pleasure, which is His heart's desire. He is a living God and very purposeful. Such a purposeful God surely has a desire. He wants something and He wants to do something, so He made a plan. This plan needs to be accomplished, and to carry out the accomplishment of this plan many works are needed. God made a plan with an arrangement to fulfill His purpose according to His desire. This plan, this arrangement, is His economy, His *oikonomia,* His household arrangement, His household administration.

In God's economy there are three steps or stages. The first step was taken by the Father, the second step was taken by the Son, and the third step was taken by the Spirit. In each step of this successive economy there are some works to be accomplished.

The Father

In the first step there was the need to exercise foreknowledge. Second, God selected persons according to His foreknowledge, and third, He predestinated or marked out His chosen people. This is according to the New Testament revelation. In the first step of God's economy, the works which were done in eternity past were all done by the Father. This does not mean, however, that when the Father did these three things, the Son was not there or the Spirit was not there. If we say this, we jeopardize the essential Trinity and the unique essence of the Trinity. In other words, we jeopardize the existence of the Triune God. This kind of interpretation leads to modalism because modalism tells us that the Father, the Son, and the Spirit have a successive existence. Their existences are in succession. When the Father was there, there was no Son or no Spirit. When the Son came, the Father was over and the Spirit was not yet. Then when the Spirit came, the Father and the Son both were over. This is the heresy of modalism. When the Father was working to exercise His foreknowledge to choose His people and to mark out His chosen ones to predestinate them unto sonship, the Son was with Him and the Spirit was with Him. He did it in the Son and with the Spirit.

The Son

After this first step of His economy, God came in firstly to create, secondly to become flesh, thirdly to live a human life on this earth, fourthly to die an all-inclusive death on the cross, fifthly to enter into resurrection, and finally to enter into ascension, the exaltation. These are the six main works in the second step of God's economy, and these works all have been done by the Son with the Father and by the Spirit. In the Bible we are told that, "all things came into being through Him, and apart from Him nothing came into being which has come into being" (John 1:3). The creating work was done by the Son for God to become flesh in Him.

For God to live a human life among the human race on this earth in a lowly family is a particular work. This does not seem so great, but no human adjective can describe this work. Too often we Christians do not think about this. We do not consider God's living on this earth in the Man Jesus for thirty-three and a half years as a great work. When people teach concerning Christ, they mostly do not stress this aspect. They stress His creation, His incarnation, His crucifixion, His resurrection, and His ascension. They skip over His human living. We must realize, however, that among His six works, the item of His human living took Him the longest time. The

Lord did not spend thirty-three and a half years to create. Also, He took only nine months to become flesh, He only took six hours to die an all-inclusive death, and He might have taken less than thirty-six hours to accomplish His resurrection. Of course, His exaltation work probably involved only a matter of minutes to accomplish. However, He took thirty-three and a half years to accomplish His human living. This is marvelous!

The major part of the revelation in the four Gospels is the human living of Jesus. His conception, His birth, His death, resurrection, and ascension are at the two ends of this revelation, while the main part is His human living. For example, in the book of Matthew, chapter one covers the Lord's conception and birth, and chapters twenty-seven and twenty-eight cover His death and resurrection. Therefore, twenty-five chapters of Matthew are on the Lord's human living. The bulk of the revelation in the four Gospels covers the human living of our Savior.

I hope that none of us, especially the young saints among us, would think that we have exhausted the New Testament. I would like to have another ten years to have a Life-study of the New Testament. Many of today's Christians merely pick up "gleanings" from the field of the divine revelation, and they become proud. This is a poor situation. Even what we have picked up from the divine revelation of the holy Word might also be considered in the Lord's eyes as "gleanings." It may be that we have not touched the harvest in the Lord's revelation. Our Life-study of the Bible, only comparatively speaking, may be the best.

Now we can see what a great, fine, and patient work was done by this One who spent thirty-three and a half years to carry out the silent work of His human living. This work has all been done by the Son. This again, however, does not mean that when the Son was doing this work the Father was absent, and the Spirit came to replace Him. This kind of understanding is modalism. The New Testament, though, tells us that whatever the Son did, He did it with the Father and by the Spirit. The Son was sent by the Father and He was even given to us by the Father, but when He came, He came with the Father. He did not only come with the Father, but He also came in the Father's name. This means that He came as the Father. If I come to the meeting in another person's name, that means I come as that person. If I go to the bank to draw some money in another person's name, I go there as that person. The bank would not call me by my name, but it would call me by that other person's name. In the same way, the Son came with the Father in the Father's name.

The Son came in a way of divine conception which was carried out by the Spirit, of the Spirit, and with the Spirit. The divine conception of Jesus was carried out by the Holy Spirit, of the Holy Spirit, and with the Holy Spirit. The Holy Spirit was the very essence of His conception. The Lord's human essence came from the virgin Mary and His divine essence came from the Holy Spirit. His conception was a mingling of the divine essence with the human essence, and this mingling produced a God-man. This was a man produced of two essences and two natures—the divine and the human. He came with the Father and He came by the Spirit. He did His work with the Father and He did His work by the Spirit. When He was baptized in the water, He was baptized with the Father and by the Spirit. When He was arrested, He was arrested with the Father and by the Spirit. When He was judged and crucified, He was judged and crucified with the Father and by the Spirit. If we do not see this, we jeopardize the existence of the Trinity. The works done by the Son were done with the Father and by the Spirit.

We have seen that Jesus was conceived of the Spirit and that the Spirit was one of His two essences. After His baptism He was standing in the water with the essence of the Holy Spirit, and, no doubt, also with the Father, yet the Spirit still came down as a dove to descend upon Him, and the Father spoke from the heavens concerning Him. This is the economical Trinity to carry out God's economy. In the same principle, when He was crucified and hanging on the cross, God forsook Him (Matt. 27:46). This does not mean that God left Him essentially, but that God left Him economically.

The Spirit

There are three steps in God's economy and each step has a certain amount of work. We have covered two steps and now we must see the third step—the step of the Spirit's application. In this step there are a great many works. After finishing the works of the second step, the Son became a life-giving Spirit. Actually, the life-giving Spirit is the issue of the work He has done in the second step. He finished incarnation, human living, His all-inclusive death, resurrection, and ascension. In resurrection He became the life-giving Spirit, and this life-giving Spirit is the issue of His incarnation, human living, death, and resurrection. This does not mean that the life-giving Spirit is a separate Spirit from the Holy Spirit. This means, however, that His death and resurrection has brought all the works He has done in the second step into the very constitution of the Spirit. Therefore, before His death "the Spirit was not yet" (John 7:39), but after His resurrection the Spirit came out with all the constituents of divinity, humanity, human living, His all-inclusive death, and His excellent resurrection. The third step, the step of the Spirit's application, is not the Spirit working with the Son but rather the Son working as the Spirit with the Father.

THE DIVINE TRINITY FOR THE DIVINE DISPENSING

According to the entire revelation of the sixty-six books of the Bible, the Trinity of the Godhead is for God's dispensing. God's desire with His strong intention is to dispense Himself into His chosen people as their life, as their life supply, and as their everything. To do this or to carry out this dispensing He needs to be triune. Without His Trinity, He has no way to carry out His divine dispensing. Therefore, His Trinity is absolutely for the divine dispensing. The first verse which clearly bears the denotation of the divine Trinity is Genesis 1:26. When God was going to create man, there should have been a council in the Godhead (as the one revealed in Acts 2:23—see note 1 there). In that conference They conversed in this way: "Let us make man in our image, after our likeness." This sounds very much like a talk in a council. In the creation of the heavens and the earth there was not such a council, such a talk, which refers to "us." The "us" is the divine Trinity—the Father, the Son, and the Spirit. The first mentioning of the divine Trinity refers to the divine dispensing. God made man in His own image and after His own likeness for the coming work of dispensing Himself into man.

When the work in the first and the second steps of His economy was accomplished, He came back to His disciples and charged them to go and disciple the nations, baptizing them into the name of the Father and of the Son and of the Holy Spirit (Matt. 28:19). This was absolutely for dispensing because by this time the very divine Trinity had been fully completed. In John 7:39 the last item of the divine Trinity was not yet, not complete. After the Lord's death and resurrection, however, the divine Trinity was fully complete and ready for God's chosen people to be baptized into for the divine dispensing. Vincent's word study tells us that the baptism referred to in Matthew 28:19 brings people into a spiritual and mystical union with the Triune God. Later I referred to this as an organic union. Baptism brings people into the Triune God, into a spiritual union with the Triune God as indicated by the word "into." This is an organic union for the divine dispensing.

Whenever we come to any verses or any expressions concerning the divine Trinity we have to be impressed with the dispensing of the divine Trinity. Ephesians 2:18 says, "For through Him we both have access in one Spirit unto the Father." The divine Trinity is mentioned in this verse for the divine dispensing. Also, in Ephesians 3:14-17 Paul tells us that he bowed his knees unto the Father that we would be strengthened with power through His Spirit into our inner man, that Christ may make His home in our hearts. This again refers to the divine Trinity for the divine dispensing. Second Corinthians 13:14 says, "The grace of the Lord Jesus Christ, and the love of God, and the fellowship of the Holy Spirit be with you all." Again in this verse we see the divine Trinity for the divine dispensing.

As we have seen, the divine Trinity is the top divine attribute of our God. In the theological study of the past concerning

God's person, the word triune was invented. Triune is an adjective just as holy is an adjective. The Triune God bears an attribute which is trinity. Just as holy produces holiness so triune produces trinity. Holiness is an attribute of God and trinity is also an attribute of God. In 2 Corinthians 13:14 grace, love, and fellowship are attributes of the Triune God, but the top attribute of our God is the Trinity. To say that He is dispensing Himself into us is a general speaking. Specifically speaking, we must realize that He is dispensing His Trinity because His Trinity is the top and all-inclusive attribute including His love, His grace, His fellowship, His holiness, and His everything.

If God were not triune, the Father, the Son, and the Spirit, He could not have a way to dispense Himself into us. Many works have been accomplished in God's economy, which consists of three steps, and this economy is the economy of the very one God who is essentially one. He performed many works. The Father exercised His foreknowledge. He chose us and predestinated us in the Son and with the Spirit. As the Son, the Triune God did many works in creation, incarnation, human living, crucifixion, resurrection, and ascension. Now He is doing a finer work as the Spirit in regeneration, sanctification, transformation, conformation, and glorification. He is also living in us and guiding us in many, many things as the Spirit.

THE ALL-INCLUSIVE DIVINE TITLE

It is always safe to use the general term of God. God chose us, God predestinated us, God created us, God became flesh, God accomplished redemption and redeemed us, God regenerated us, God sanctified us, and God is doing everything in us, through us, and for us. God is the all-inclusive divine title. To use this all-inclusive, divine title is always right. To use the subsidiary divine titles such as the Father, the Son, and the Spirit, we must be careful.

There is nothing wrong with saying that God exercised His foreknowledge, chose us, predestinated us, and created the world. God also became flesh and accomplished redemption. He regenerated us and He is sanctifying us and guiding us.

We cannot say, however, that the Son selected us and that the Spirit predestinated us. Neither can we say that the Father became flesh, died on the cross for our sins, resurrected, and ascended. Acts 20:28 tells us that God purchased the church with His own blood. We can say in a general way that God purchased or redeemed the church. We cannot say, however, that the Father purchased us. In the Bible we cannot see the church of the Father or the church of the Spirit, but the church of Christ and the church of God. The Father, however, has regenerated us because His function as a Father is begetting. We may say that the Son regenerates us as the Spirit, but we cannot say that the Spirit redeems us. We also cannot say that the Spirit created the world. Neither can we say that the Spirit selected us. Now we must ask who redeems our body? Philippians 3:21 indicates that the Lord Jesus Christ, the Son, will transfigure us.

THE BIBLE—CONSTRUCTED WITH THE TRINITY

This fellowship may help you to realize how to use, understand, and apply many verses in the Bible, especially in the New Testament, concerning the divine Trinity because as a whole the Bible is constructed with the divine Trinity. This is a great subject. I believe that if we are faithful to Him in the coming years, more light will come concerning this matter. I expect that our fellowship in this chapter will help us to understand and experience the divine Trinity more easily.

THE NEED OF
AN ADEQUATE KNOWLEDGE OF THE TRUTH

We have only touched a small amount of the truth in the Bible. To some extent we have wasted people's time and held them back because we did not know the truth adequately. Year after year we nearly presented the same thing to people. We must realize that the basic problem is the problem of not having the adequate knowledge of the basic truth. Because we are short of the adequate knowledge of the truth, we are influenced by "good things." An adequate knowledge of the truth can preserve us. Throughout church history, Christendom has picked up many things which are not in accordance with the truth of the divine revelation. Once the adequate knowledge of the truth came in, many of these things were dropped and "mopped away." Up until Luther's time, the Catholic Church had picked up much "dirt" of pagan practices and unscriptural doctrines. Then Luther stood up to put out one basic truth—justification by faith. This truth swept away a lot of dirt. The Catholic Church became "dirty" because of the lack of knowledge of the truth. If I discover any dirt, it is my responsibility to sweep it away with the truth. Many of us have an inadequate knowledge of the Lord's recovery. This means you are short of protection and you miss the safeguard. We must clean up the dirt, not by human doing, but by presenting the truth. Once the saints see the truth, they know where they are, and they know what the Lord's recovery is.

CHAPTER NINE

BRINGING THE SAINTS INTO THE TRUTH

(1)

GETTING INTO THE MINISTRY

Thus far, we have seen that to carry out this New Testament ministry we must first get into this ministry. After getting into it, we must have some proper way or the best way to help the saints in the recovery to get solidly educated in this New Testament ministry. I believe that when all the saints in the recovery have received the proper education they will spontaneously become good ministers to carry such a ministry to the outsiders, to the unbelievers, and to the other Christians who do not meet with us. I feel that it is crucial for us to find out what the best way is to help the saints in each local church to get into the same things which we ourselves have gotten into.

MEETINGS OF EDUCATION

I believe that this will affect the way of our meeting, so we have to consider or reconsider the way of our meeting. We must find the best way to turn our meetings into meetings of education. The saints who are meeting with us all the time need to be educated. Based upon our experience over the years, we must admit that in the matter of educating the saints we have not been very successful. A number of the saints have been meeting with us for years and years, but they still have not gotten into the basic intrinsic element of the Lord's recovery. We all have to admit that from the point of view of educating the saints with the basic truth our way of meeting has not been so successful. We surely do not appreciate the way today's

Christians have their meetings. Many of us, including myself, have attended Christian meetings from our youth. For many years I attended the services, heard the sermons, and went to Sunday school, but nearly nothing got into me. However, something of the Bible stories and of the traditional Christian practices surely got into me, and I became that kind of Christian. Actually, no truth, no life, no Spirit, or no reality had ever gotten into me. I believe that we all have to admit that a good number of saints have been meeting with us year after year, yet if you check with them today, you would discover that not much intrinsic element of the divine revelation has been really wrought and constituted into their being. Not only in the matter of life but even more in the matter of the truth not much intrinsic element has been wrought into the saints. I am really concerned that not many among us can present particular truths in an adequate way.

READING THE LIFE-STUDIES

I recently discovered that at least some of you probably have never read over fifty Life-study messages. This is according to my observation and some information which came to me. Occasionally information came to me spontaneously which I did not expect. Actually, to some extent, I did not like to hear these things. I am not a person who desires to hear others' situations. However, I must say honestly to some of you that by your direct contact with me, I realized that you had not read many of the Life-studies. If you had, you would not have talked to me in the way that you did. I have the full confidence in the working out of the Life-study messages. I do not believe that anyone who had read between two hundred and five hundred Life-study messages could have talked to me in that way. Your talk to me exposed yourselves. Let me give an example from my experience in learning English to further clarify this matter. I learned English mainly in writing and not in speaking. Since I came to America, you all can testify that by my speaking over the years I have improved in speaking the English language. By my speaking all of you can realize where I stand and how much labor I have spent in learning how to speak the English language. In like manner, when you come to me, your talk exposes to me where you are as far as the truth is concerned.

A PARTICULAR COMMISSION

Under the Lord's mercy I came to this country with a particular commission, a particular burden, to bring the Lord's recovery to the top Christian country. I fully realized the responsibility and the hardship involved, yet I would not avert from this commission, and I came with a burden to present the truth. After a few years of being here in the United States, I fully realized that the truths were not properly or adequately understood in a deeper way in this country.

Brother Nee indicated to me definitely that the United States was hopeless concerning the Lord's truth. He said that superficiality and worldliness were the two main factors for this. He indicated that Britain and Germany were solid countries, but that the United States was loose and too worldly. Also Brother Nee never agreed for any young saints among us to come to the United States. He never encouraged this. He indicated that if anyone wanted to go out to study, they should go to England. I received such an impression from Brother Nee and I came to the United States with a burden. I found out, of course, that the situation was not exactly the same as what Brother Nee had told me. I found out that the people here are not that superficial and are not that loose. However, I did discover that not many of the deeper truths were really understood by the seeking Christians in a solid way. As a result my burden was to bring the Lord's recovery to the United States. After staying in the United States for two years, I had a burden to present the truth, trying my best to hold conferences and to visit many cities. From 1962 to 1974 I went to many places presenting the truth. By 1974 I realized that merely to present the truth with subjects and certain topics would not be an adequate way. Therefore, I began to bear the burden to put out Life-study messages on the books of the Bible in a very good sequence.

The highlight of all the conferences was in 1973. Before this time the highest attendance we had at a conference was approximately twelve hundred, but in the summer conference of 1973 the attendance went up to over three thousand. Suddenly the number more than doubled. So many coming to the conference helped me to make the decision to change from a conference way to a training way. There is no control with a conference because it is open to the entire public. We cannot reject anyone who wants to come to a conference. A training, however, is in the nature of a school, and there is the need for people to be registered. By 1974 there was the need to put out the truth according to the sequence of the books of the Bible, and there was also the need to have some registration to control the attendance so that the standard of those attending would not be so low. Therefore, the decision was made to have annual trainings twice a year. We have seen to some extent that the registration for the training has been a kind of restriction. The standard has been raised up and the atmosphere in the meetings has been very much adjusted and improved. You also realize that in the trainings I have the freedom to say things to you that I would not have in a conference.

THE PURPOSE OF THE RECOVERY VERSION
WITH THE NOTES

To Present the Truth

In 1974 I began to write the notes for the Recovery Version of the Bible. I have written these notes to expound the books of the Bible for a few purposes. The main purpose is to bring you into the truth. As of January of 1985, we had trainings over the entire twenty-seven books of the New Testament. Those of you who have been trainees in the trainings should have realized that the first purpose of the notes of the Recovery Version is to present the truth. I do not believe you can find as many basic truths in other books as you have found in the Recovery Version. Other expositions and commentaries, for example, do not correctly point out what the main truth in the book of Matthew is. The Recovery Version clearly points out that this is a book on the kingdom of the heavens and it gives you a proper definition of the truths concerning the kingdom of the heavens.

To Minister the Life Supply

The first purpose of the notes is to present to you the truth, and the second purpose is to minister to you the life supply. Many of you can testify that you do not get as much nourishment from other expositions and commentaries as you can from the Recovery Version.

To Solve the Common and Hard Problems in the New Testament

The third purpose of the notes is to help us to solve the common and hard problems in the New Testament. In nearly every book of the New Testament there are some questions which are hard to answer and some problems and points which are hard to understand. The notes in the Recovery Version are also an attempt to solve the hard problems in the Bible to help the readers get through them. I have had much experience as a young man studying the Bible. I came to a certain point in the Bible that I could not understand and I became stuck on that point. For instance, 2 Peter 2:4 refers to the gloomy pits to which the angels who sinned were delivered. When I read this in the Chinese version as a young man I got stuck on this point. I did not know what the Chinese meant by a gloomy pit. In the Recovery Version, however, there are adequate notes to help on problems such as these (see note 4^2 in 2 Peter 2 and note 19^3 in 1 Peter 3). For problems such as these in the Bible, I spend much time to go to the original Greek, to the lexicons, to the concordances, and to others' expositions in order to get a proper understanding. By the Lord's mercy, I believe and thank the Lord that I received such an understanding. Therefore, for each of these problems I have given you a proper interpretation to help you to understand them properly. This means to remove all the obstacles on your "driveway" that you may have a clear route and highway for a drive in your Bible study. Today we have a Recovery Version of the New Testament with nearly no obstacles on the driving way. You can drive your "study car" through any book of the New Testament without stops. If you have a problem you can refer to the notes for help.

To Open Up the Books of the Bible

The fourth purpose of the Recovery Version with the notes is to open up the books of the Bible. After the Recovery Version of a book had been published, that particular book of the Bible was opened to us. Because we have a Recovery Version of the entire New Testament, we must testify that the books of the New Testament have been opened to us. We have an open book. Some teachers of the Bible admit that Revelation is a closed book and that it is too deep. Also, a number of believers were told not to touch Revelation and to stay away from it. To most believers Revelation is a closed book, but when you get the Recovery Version of Revelation you cannot say that it is a closed book. It is an open book. The Recovery Version of Revelation gives you a very brief and concise interpretation of the book.

I have made an attempt to open every book of the New Testament to you, but I have left the further digging to you. I have only "opened up the mine," and I have not dug that much. The foundation which Brother Watchman Nee laid in China helped me greatly. During his time, however, he told me that the Lord had not permitted him to write any expositions. Through the messages I heard personally and directly from him, through the publications put out by him, and through many direct talks with him for over at least eighteen years, I received a very solid foundational word to build on. As a result, I picked up the burden to write the expository notes for the Recovery Version to open each book of the New Testament to the seeking saints. Both Brother Nee and I did not have that much time to dig further. I want to dig further and I am still digging, but I do not believe that I can do that much. Therefore, I leave this further digging matter to you.

The basic truths have been presented to us, and much life nourishment has been put into print, especially with the Life-study messages. Also, the obstacles have nearly all been removed. We now have a clear way for our study, and every book is open to us. In mining, the hardest thing is to open the mine. Once the mine has been opened and the treasure is exposed, it is easy for someone to dig out the treasures. I have left only this one matter of further digging to you. I believe the Lord will continue this digging work either through you or through some others. After a period of time I believe that many of you will be "good diggers." The intention and the goal of our publishing of the Life-study messages is to open up the mine for you to go in and dig.

A TEXTBOOK FOR STUDY

In order to get the benefit of these four purposes in full you must dive into the Recovery Version with the footnotes and the Life-study messages. It is not an easy task to be built up in the truth. You must study the text and every note. If possible, it is helpful to take care of the cross-references. Then you need to study the Life-study messages. You need to get into these messages not like you are reading a newspaper or a reference book. You must consider the text of the Recovery Version with the notes and the Life-study messages as a textbook. Because this is my work, I know the nature of it. I am fellowshipping this with you to let you know the way our publications were written. If you merely read them in a light way, you cannot get into them. You must study them as a textbook.

If you merely read the Life-studies, you will only receive a temporary nourishment. That will only become a kind of inspiration to you. An inspiration is like a vapor in the air. When what we read becomes a truth in our being, this nourishment remains forever. What I have received is not all the time inspiration, like a vapor. What I have received from the Lord is always the solid truth, so it remains in me, nourishing me all the time. You must have the truth. The only way for the truth to get into you is through your mentality. Then it remains in your memory. If you do not understand, the truth cannot get into you. The truth gets into you through your mentality, your understanding. Also, if the truth gets into your memory, it becomes a constant and long term nourishment. Then you have an accumulation of the truth, and you are a person continually under the constant nourishment. You will then know how to present the truth to others, not merely to inspire them or to stir them up, but to make them solid and constituted with the truth.

THE WAY TO MEET

I do not have any definite decision as to what way we should take with our church meetings. If I were taking care of a local church meeting, I would not make any decision immediately. I would go into the meetings and by going on in the meeting life I would learn something. I would realize what the best way is to have a meeting. We may begin to have an experimental period of time to gradually find out what the best way is.

First, we must admit that the type of meetings today among the Christians on this earth is altogether inadequate. I do not believe that any meeting among the Christians today on this earth corresponds with some of the meetings under Paul's leadership in the New Testament times. We have no record of these meetings and we cannot trace them, but I do believe that even the meetings we practice do not correspond that much to the meetings which were at Paul's time. I believe the Lord did this because this age is an age of life and of the Spirit, even of the sevenfold intensified Spirit, not of letters, rituals, or forms. I believe the Lord intentionally did not let us know what the way was, because once He would let us know the way, it would become a fixed ritual. Today there is no Christian that can tell us what the fixed way for Christian meetings is. Therefore, we have to grope for the proper way by our spirit according to the present, real situation. We may also discuss some principles. We hope that the leading ones, either the elders or the ones who are taking care of any meeting such as the Chinese speaking meetings, the Spanish speaking meetings, and the young people's meetings, would pick up a burden and look to the Lord for a desire that all the saints would get into this New Testament ministry.

ACQUIRING A SOLID KNOWLEDGE
OF THE NEW TESTAMENT MINISTRY

We have seen that to get ourselves into the New Testament ministry needs time. We must mean business with the Lord. I became full-time in the Lord's work in 1933. Before 1933, immediately after I was saved, was mainly my college education period. I studied in school and after graduation I had a job, but morning and evening and especially on Saturdays and the Lord's Day I did nothing but study the Bible. I would not call the books that I studied spiritual books, but books concerning the understanding of the Bible. I mostly received an education concerning the Bible from the Brethren assembly meetings. They did not care for how many were there in their meeting. They only cared for one thing— to pass on the knowledge of the Bible. At that time I greatly appreciated them and they treasured me because as a young man I was a continuous attendant of their meetings. What I heard in their meetings and what I read in the books I studied.

I spent at least eight years building a basic foundational knowledge of the Bible before I came out as a full-time worker. I have had altogether seven Chinese Bibles. I lost the first Bible, but I have the other six. The second Bible is full of notes, but they are very childish. The fourth Bible, however, is worthwhile to use and has more notes which are much more mature. This Bible is greatly worn out. If I could have had today's Recovery Version with the notes and the Life-study messages at my time, that would have been wonderful. In those eight years, though, I surely got into the knowledge of the Bible.

This is what I expect of you brothers who are taking the lead in the church or in any kind of meeting. You must acquire a solid knowledge of the New Testament ministry. What I got into as a young man was good but it was far off. There was nothing of the Triune God dispensing Himself, nothing of Christ and the church, and nothing of Christ, the Spirit, life, and the church. At that time I acquired much biblical knowledge concerning prophecy and typology. I also received the benefit of learning how to interpret prophecy. The Brethren assembly teachers were famous in knowing the Bible, and no other groups could compete with them. Even today the reference books which I use cannot compete with J. N. Darby. No one can present any principle in knowing the Bible as deeply as Darby. Darby's five volumes of the *Synopsis of the Books of the Bible* bear a particular characteristic in that he presented the principles for understanding the Bible.

In 1925 I wrote Brother Nee asking him to please tell me what book could help me to understand the entire Bible. He said that according to his knowledge the best one is J. N. Darby's *Synopsis of the Books of the Bible*. He wrote this to me fifty-nine years ago, and he told me that I needed to read these volumes anywhere from three to five times; otherwise, he indicated that I would not be able to understand them. I can testify that without reading Darby three to five times, you do not know what he is talking about. Sometimes one sentence of his is equivalent to a long paragraph. He has the ability to put phrase after phrase and clause after clause into a sentence. I have been influenced by him to some extent in my writing. Sometimes to make two or three sentences out of one long sentence changes the denotation.

LABORING TO GET INTO THE MINISTRY

You must get into the New Testament ministry. Some of you may be concerned as to how you could do this. In spite of this, you must do it. Today all the people in Houston at NASA are taking care of the exploration of space. Many of these people have doctor's degrees and are working day and night. Otherwise, they could never have gotten such a position. If the worldly people can work this hard for worldly things, what about us? We should consider our business as the King's business. Our job is much higher than their job. How could we do our business lightly? We could not. Some of you have considered the Lord's recovery too lightly. You never got into the Recovery Version and you have never read more than fifty Life-study messages, even though about twelve hundred Life-study messages have been published. Yet you still consider that you know something. I do not mean that you do not know anything, but you must realize that, even humanly speaking, a short period of study does not qualify a person to get a job having to do with the exploration of space in the space center in Houston. Some of you have been in the recovery for years and yet you have never gotten into the intrinsic element of the Lord's recovery. We must consider that what the Lord has shown us over the years is not that shallow.

I came to this country with a burden to present the solid truth. I realize that I have been a little limited, especially because English is not my mother tongue. Still, I have published many things which need your spending years to get into. If you think this is something so easy for you to get into, you are wrong. You need years to get into the New Testament ministry. I do not think that you are such a genius that you can do a quicker job than I did. To put out the things of the ministry has required me to labor both day and night for years. Even during this training while I have been speaking here three times a day I have studied much in the morning and in the night. I still study the Word daily. Some of your talk to me, however, showed me that you did not spend that much time to get into the ministry. Through your talk I realized that you did not read or study the Life-studies.

OUR MEETINGS—LIVING, NOURISHING, AND EDUCATING

We have come to a point in the Lord's recovery where we must consider how to meet. Our way of meeting is related to how to use the Life-study messages. In other words, we must find out the best way to carry out the New Testament ministry. In principle, I feel that we, the leaders, must get into the ministry and we must find a way to bring our congregation into it. I do not feel, however, that we should conduct our meetings like classes in the schools. We do not want to have a meeting to teach the saints the things in the Life-studies in a dead way. We must, by the Lord's grace, keep our meetings so living and so full of nourishment. But still, we must carry out the saints' education in the basic truths. Then all the saints who have been meeting in the Lord's recovery with us for many years will get the adequate, solid, and basic education of the New Testament economy. Eventually, they will have the New Testament ministry to minister these truths to the unbelievers, to the believers who do not meet with us, and also to minister life to all the people. We should not, however, have any intention to proselyte people. Our burden should simply be to preach the gospel, to teach the truth, and to minister life to people. This is our commission. When the Lord was on this earth He also preached the gospel, taught the truth, ministered life, and prepared the disciples. Millions of people received the benefit. There were not too many, however, who took the New Testament way. I feel that we should do the same thing. Then we would not be narrow or sectarian in reality.

Our meeting should be carried out in a living way such that all the saints might be nourished on the one hand and educated on the other hand. Many saints have been meeting with us for over five years and yet they do not know much concerning the basic truths. We need a new start. After three years of meeting with us, the saints should have received some solid education of the New Testament ministry. Then they will become ministers. I once said that all of us could be apostles, prophets, evangelists, shepherds and teachers. Eventually, however, we did not have the proper practice to bring all the saints into such a ministry. Time has shown us that we have to wake up. I do not blame the past since it was also quite good. We did experience the Lord's mercy, but we still need some improvement. To see something short or weak in the past does not mean that we blame that, but it means that we have to improve.

We should seek after the Lord's leading in this matter. I do not like to make any kind of legal decision that from now on every local church has to take certain kinds of steps in a legal way. Maybe one local church has a sense to take a certain way and another local church takes a little different way. Only the Lord knows. We must, however, pick up the principles that govern us and we must have some basic points to work on. How to carry out the meetings depends on the environment of your location and the need of your congregation. In principle, we need thorough fellowship, and then the Lord may lead us to pick up a better way to take care of our meetings. This does not necessarily mean that we would revolutionize and completely change our meetings. My intention is not to belittle or lower down our meetings in the past but to uplift them. I believe the Lord has brought us to the highest plane and at the least the high place, but we still need some improvement. Pray about this.

CHAPTER TEN

BRINGING THE SAINTS INTO THE TRUTH

(2)

THE NEED OF THE TRUTH
TO BUILD THE CHURCH

History has clearly shown us that the existence of a denomination, free group, or the genuine church life all depends on the doctrines. If there are no doctrines, there is no church. Since the Lord's recovery has come to the United States, we have stressed very much that the building up of the church depends upon the experience of Christ, upon the life-giving Spirit, and upon the matters of life. Seemingly, I am saying something different now, but in the past I occasionally indicated that the Pentecostal movement could never have anything built up. The Assembly of God, the solid and big denomination built up by the Pentecostal movement, was established in 1914. After fifty years of their existence in 1965, I heard that through their practice they had learned to charge their theological students not to go out with the expectation that the so-called Pentecostal gifts could build up the church. They charged their students to realize that the way to build up the church is to put out doctrines or teachings. Therefore, in the Assembly of God meetings they do not practice speaking in tongues. Mainly, they preach the gospel and teach the doctrines for edifying the saints. This does not mean that they gave up the speaking in tongues, but that they exercise these gifts in their private lives.

I say this to show you that even in the past I occasionally indicated strongly that the so-called "Spirit" cannot build up the church, but the solid truth or the solid doctrines can.

Certainly, what kind of church you will build up depends upon what kind of truth you teach. Since 1962 here in the United States we have stressed greatly that the churches are built up not by mere doctrines but by Christ, by the Spirit, and by life. Since 1962 a great many messages have been put out on the truth. If we had not put out any messages on the truth since the recovery came to this country and we had merely learned to pray and to exercise in the gifts such as tongues and healings, today's situation would be very poor. In the past, we practiced in this way for a short time, and we found out that the issue was poor. Through the years, however, we have stressed Christ, the Spirit, and life. In all the messages what we condemned was the empty, dead doctrines of dead letters. However, we fully realized that to produce the church, to have the church exist, and to build up the church we needed to put out the solid, living truths full of Christ, full of the Spirit, and full of life. God's way to carry out His economy is to use His holy Word.

Suppose that on this earth among the human race there had never been such a book as the Bible. If we had not had a Bible in our hands during the past 2,000 years since the Lord Jesus resurrected and ascended to the heavens, everything would be in the air and nothing could be solid. Even the things concerning the Spirit could not be solid. The Spirit depends upon the Word. This is why the Lord said that the words that He spoke to us are spirit (John 6:63). The words which the Lord speaks are the solid spirit. Without the Word the Spirit is not so solid. Without the Word the Spirit might be just "a phantom." Today, however, we have the Bible. In innumerable instances we have seen that whenever people contact the holy Word, many times they get the Spirit, but it is hard to give an instance where people touch the Spirit and then they get the Word. There are a great many instances, however, which show us that when you touch the Word you get the Spirit. This is history. A principle has been set up through history that there is the desperate need of the living truth to produce the church, to help the church exist, and to build up the church.

THE LIFE-STUDIES AND RECOVERY VERSION

Through the past ten years up to the present time it has been fully proven among us that the most profitable writings and publications are the Life-study messages with the notes of the Recovery Version. I wrote these things, not for scholarly study for people to get a degree, but for life ministering, for truth releasing, and for opening up the books of the Bible. We do not need scholarly writings or any kind of books that build up peoples' degree. That is not our purpose. To some extent, we would not agree with this. We are not for theology, but we are for "theos," God. Our publications are not for any kind of "ology," but just for God, the Triune God, the processed Triune God, and the Lord, Christ, Jesus, the Spirit, life, and the church. Our publications are for a living Person, not for any "ology." We are not for the ology of God, the ology of Christ, the ology of the church, or the ology of the divine things. However, I do have a burden to publish things full of Christ, full of the Triune, processed God, full of the life-giving Spirit, full of life, and full of the church. The Lord's recovery is just for the recovery of the processed Triune God to be dispensed into us, and the living Christ, the Spirit, life, and the church are the crucial contents of the Lord's recovery. There is no other place to pick up other books which are so rich, so enlightening, and so nourishing concerning the recovery of Christ, the Spirit, life, and the church. Since this is the real situation and the real condition, I feel that we have no choice but to use the Life-studies, because we realize that this is the best way to bring people into the holy Word.

The holy Word itself says in Psalm 119:130: "The entrance of thy words giveth light." Millions of copies of the Bible have been distributed. They have been placed in hotels, in homes, and in many places. Nearly everywhere you go today you find a Bible, but who has entered into the Bible? There has nearly been no entrance. Many have a copy of the Bible, but the Bible has been closed and nearly never opened. Now the Lord has given us a key, an opener. I consider our writings as the opener to open the holy Word. I believe that those of you who have read the Life-study messages can testify honestly that these messages with the notes of the Recovery Version have opened up a certain chapter or a certain book of the Bible to you. This is not to replace the Bible but to bring people into the Bible.

BRINGING THE SAINTS INTO THE TRUTH

Based upon this, I feel that for the long range for the Lord's recovery in such a top country as the United States, which is full of culture, education, scientific knowledge, and biblical knowledge, the greatest need we must meet is to bring the saints in the Lord's recovery into the truth to carry the Lord's recovery on. For a country to be strong there is the need to bring its people into the proper education. If the people are behind in education, that country is also behind. The reason why the United States is a top country is because of its highest education. When President Nixon was in office, he encouraged the young people to study at the universities because many young Americans at that time did not want to study further after high school. The trend in the United States has changed, however. Such a big country needs many more people to receive the highest, up-to-date education. Otherwise, there is no way for a country to be among the top countries in today's world.

Today we are here for the Lord's recovery. For the long run, we surely have to help the saints in the Lord's recovery to get into the top spiritual education. You must remember that we still uplift the living Christ, the life-giving Spirit, life itself and its riches, and the church in a living way. To promote these things, to carry these things out, and to bring people into these things so that they remain there, we need the Word and we need the truth. The standard of the Lord's recovery depends upon the standard of the truth we put out. The truths will be the measure and the standard.

Some may think that I am "selling my cargo." They may also think that I am controlling so that no other teaching would come into the Lord's recovery. I want to make the real situation clear to all of you. After four or five years, some better things may come out. I cannot predict and only the Lord knows. If that would happen, we had better go to take these better things. I would take the lead to take them. While I am writing the notes and putting out the messages, I am always on the alert to see if anything new has come out. Many Christian publications are produced in the United States; in other countries, however, there has nearly been nothing produced. What spiritual publications have come out in the past twenty years in France or Russia? What spiritual publications have come out of Britain in recent times? Britain was used by the Lord greatly in the last century. The saints there really saw something, and groups of great Bible teachers were produced in Britain up to the first third of this century. After the first third of this century, however, Britain has produced nearly nothing in the way of top spiritual publications. From my observation, nearly nothing has come out of Germany in recent years. In the past twenty years since the Lord's recovery came to the United States, the only things that I can see which have been produced by Christians of some worth and value have been from the United States. In the past twenty years the Christians in the United States have put out a number of books, such as lexicons, Greek concordances, and word-studies of the Scriptures. These books are very good and I encourage you all to buy them. However, there has been nothing published in the way of exposition that is worthwhile. It is good for us to purchase the books on the Greek and Hebrew languages since these are very useful. The best choice for exposition, however, is to use our publications.

We need to find a way to bring all the saints in the Lord's recovery into a proper education of the truth concerning God's New Testament economy. We need to consider this matter in two aspects—the personal aspect and the meeting aspect. We must have a personal way laid as a foundation for us to stand on and then go on to take care of the meeting way.

THE NEED OF A SOLID FOUNDATION IN THE WORD

The Lord's recovery has been in the United States for over twenty years. During this time, all those who left the church and who caused trouble and became a failure never received a solid foundation in the Word. Everyone in the past twenty years who has passed through all kinds of tests and who was not only never shaken but also never affected are a real benefit to the Lord's recovery. Whatever the storm was they remained steadfast and they went on with the Lord and are still here. They have not been a damage or a problem. Everyone like this is one that loves the Word and has a sound foundation in the truth. There is not an exception to this either on the positive side or on the negative side. All those who became a problem never had a solid foundation in the Word.

Over the last ten years we have published approximately twelve hundred Life-studies. I have the assurance to say that whoever has read through five hundred Life-study messages properly has been an excellent believer. You elders who are shepherding the local churches know the real situation of most of the saints. If a saint in your locality is not that "proper" and he would begin from tomorrow morning to read the Life-study messages until he reaches five hundred, he will become another person. Medicine, nourishment, and all kinds of vitamins are included in these messages. This is why I said earlier that I had some realization that some of the saints who contacted me had not read many of the Life-studies. I realized that they had not taken the "medicine and nourishment." In their talk there were symptoms and signs of sickness. For example, a doctor may prescribe certain drugs for his patient. When the patient comes back to him after two months, the doctor can tell whether or not the patient took the drugs. The patient's breathing, color, and entire being tells the doctor that the patient did not take the prescription. If you would begin to study the Life-studies every day starting tomorrow morning, you will become a different person even after fifty days.

By the Lord's mercy, I am quite healthy. I am doing much more than what I did in the past. When I was in Shanghai, I never spoke twice a day. I only spoke once a day at the most, and I did not do as much writing work as I do today. My wife always reminds me that I am eighty years old now and that sixty-five is the age of retirement. She tells me I am doubling my work instead of retiring. My point is this—the reason that

I am quite healthy is because I eat the healthy food. After speaking for two sessions in one of the morning meetings of this training, I was tired. I went back home, ate lunch, and laid down. I then rested until five and became refreshed. Then I ate another meal and came to the evening meeting to minister the Word. In the evening I spoke until nine-thirty. After the evening meeting I went home, ate a snack, and slept well. After eating in the morning I was refreshed and invigorated. The reason for this is a good diet full of the proper nourishment.

I have the assurance that if you would get into the Life-study messages continually, you will be different after fifty days. Any message from any book, such as Genesis, Exodus, Matthew, or Revelation, is good for your study. Just go to the Life-study messages. I hope that the Lord would really have mercy upon us that we do not hold any kind of personal feeling or individualistic opinion. We must be those who solely take care of the interest of the Lord's recovery and the benefit of all the dear saints who have come into the Lord's recovery. We only care for this.

We must do our best to get ourselves into these truths and to get these truths constituted into our being. This cannot be done within a short time, but this must be our practice. I also am burdened that all the leading ones, either the elders or the serving ones taking some kind of lead, should have a real burden to pray for the saints in your locality that the Lord may stir up their interest, their seeking heart, and their spirit to seek after the Lord in His truth. The truth is nowhere but in the Bible, yet the Bible needs an opener. We need to lead the saints into the real, right, and proper realization of the need of the Bible and also of the help of the Life-study messages and the Recovery Version.

BUILDING UP A HABIT
OF SPENDING TIME IN THE WORD

We should help the saints to build up a practice or a habit that every day they would spend at least thirty minutes in the Word. This can be done by taking ten minutes in the morning, ten minutes in the evening, and another ten minutes before going to bed. We all need to build up such a practice to spend at least thirty minutes a day to get into God's Word. The best way is to charge the saints to study a book of the New Testament according to their choice. They should get into this book continually and every day. Some saints may decide to study the book of Romans or the book of Hebrews. They should study every day either three times of ten minutes each or one time of thirty minutes. We should charge them to pray-read two or three verses of this book every day. Then they have to study the accompanying message. We have messages on all the verses. The saints do not need to pray-read the Life-study messages, but they have to pray-read the biblical verses in order to get the help to enter into the truth conveyed in these few verses. They also need the help of the notes and the Life-study messages to enter into the truth. The saints need to take this way every day to get into the truth. After one year of studying the Bible in this way, there will be a solid change in the saints' home life, private life, and church life. A few verses seems very slow but we must realize that breathing is a slow thing. We only breath a little at a time, but this continual practice accumulates and keeps us living. We may think this is too slow, but even if it took us ten years to finish the entire New Testament that would be wonderful. To pick up the truth contained in half of the New Testament after five years would be marvelous. We do not encourage the saints to be greedy and attempt to finish one book in one day. Then "their stomach will burst." We should not encourage them in this way. Rather, we should slow them down. It is not a matter of quantity but a matter of endurance. You must endure this kind of Bible study. I think we need to remind them week after week, and sometimes the elders need to give the saints some direction, some encouragement, and some incentive.

THE NEED OF A PROPER DIET

Many of you leading ones have never encouraged the saints in the last five years to get into the truths in the way of using the Life-studies. You leave the matter of the saints' getting into the Life-studies altogether up to them. You do not seem to care whether this is a dying matter or a living matter. This way of getting into the truth has become an orphan with no father and no mother, with no fostering. This has been the situation, and in some of the local churches, your problems all have been due to this one thing. As a family you did not feed your folks, your children, with the proper diet. How do you expect your family to be healthy? If your family does not have the proper diet, be prepared for disease, sickness, and trouble. Do not try to solve the problems by any other way. They will not work. The only way that works is to come back to the proper diet, to feed your family with the proper food.

Some of you had the feeling that the attendance to the meetings using the Life-study messages was reducing. Then you changed the content of the meeting to the so-called new beginners' lessons. When I heard that this was your practice, I was anticipating that you would eventually have some trouble. I realized that the saints would starve. I was the first one who got charged to carry meetings with the new beginners' lessons in 1948, and I tasted the real situation. It was absolutely not suitable to carry a meeting. Every time we practiced using the new beginners' lessons for the meeting we failed. Since we have tasted failure time after time, why would we go back to this? When this report came to me I was really bothered, but I did not say a word.

The church in your locality is your family. Even if I am your grandfather that is still your family. I did not like to say anything, but I was waiting for news that you would come to me for help. I anticipated this, and now you have the trouble as a result of your diet. I cannot cure or heal you by just one visit. No visit can heal you. You must come back to the proper diet and charge your children to take the proper diet. Do not only ask them, but charge them. All the mothers in a family charge their little ones to eat properly. At every meal a proper mother charges her children to eat sufficiently and properly. In like manner, you should charge the saints to have a proper diet. You will see whether they will be healthy or not. We must realize that to shepherd a church is to take care of a big family with many folks who are young, old, and middle-aged. We must feed them properly, and we must consider what is the most nourishing, healing, and germ-killing diet. We have to make a choice.

Please do not think that I am "selling my cargo." I beg you to forget this thought which comes from the Devil. I am not selling my cargo, but I am ministering the divine truth to God's people. Therefore, as leading brothers try your best in your locality to stir up an atmosphere and to create a hunger and thirst in the saints after the Lord's truth. Tell them that the truth is in the unique holy Word and that the best help to usher them into the Word is the Recovery Version with the notes and all the Life-studies. Of course, we should not practice anything legal. We should not make these things a legal matter that the saints are required to do. However, if the saints do love the Lord's recovery, they must get themselves fed all the time with the healthy food that they may be strong. As a result of eating a proper, regular diet, the saints will be strong and the Lord will have a strong testimony.

Chapter Eleven

BRINGING THE SAINTS INTO THE TRUTH

(3)

THE MEETINGS

In this chapter we will continue our fellowship on how to bring the saints in our locality into the truth so that they will get a solid foundation in the Word. We have seen that the first aspect is the personal aspect. Each saint must have a proper, daily, regular diet of a few verses in the Bible with the notes of the Recovery Version accompanied by the Life-study messages. Now we must go on to see the second aspect, the meeting aspect.

The Basic Factor—the Spirit

We should never forget that the basic factor for our meetings should be the Spirit. The meetings should be in the Spirit. They should be full of life and full of living prayer to bring in a living atmosphere which is full of freedom for everyone to function. We must keep and have these few basic factors in all of the church meetings—full of the Spirit, full of life, full of prayer, full of a refreshing atmosphere that encourages people to function, and full of freedom for people to function. The elders and all the ones who take the lead in any kind of meeting should bear the responsibility to pray for this. An elder should not come to the meeting without a proper time of prayer for the meeting. Every elder should come to the meeting after some prayer for the meeting and come into the meeting with a praying spirit. That makes your meeting different.

To be an elder is not a small thing. The children may just

sit down at the table and expect something to be served to them. The mother, however, cannot practice in this way. Before sitting down she should have done a lot of things. Then the entire family can feed on a proper meal. Furthermore, when the church reaches a certain size, at least one or two elders should be full time. This becomes a scientific principle because when the elders are too busy or too greatly occupied with their business or with their jobs, it is hard for them to bear the responsibility of the church meetings adequately. I do not mean, however, that you prepare yourself to come to the meeting to dominate, to control, or to conduct. This is wrong. Do not prepare yourself to come to the meeting to conduct the meeting or to control the meeting. You must, however, prepare yourself to come in to bear the meeting. The meeting is just like the ark in the ancient times. The Levites bore the ark on their shoulders just like the palanquin in the Song of Songs. The elders should be those bearing the palanquin of Christ. This makes a difference. The church meetings should not be just a Bible-study class, but full of the Spirit, full of life, full of prayer, full of the fresh atmosphere, and full of freedom for everyone to open their mouths to speak forth Christ. This must be basic.

How to Carry Out the Meetings

If we could bear a meeting in such a way, I would propose that we look at the situation of the present condition of the church in our locality to determine what the present need is. The Lord may lead you to pick up a certain book such as John, Matthew, or Mark. In the church meetings it would be good to continue on a certain book and to go through it chapter after chapter. The principle for the meetings is the same as with your personal study. Some elements, of course, must be very different from our personal study. Undoubtedly, we have to pray-read the basic verses in the meeting, but the leaders and the elders should not let the pray-reading go too long. If the pray-reading is too long at the opening time of the meeting, it kills the meeting. Therefore, the pray-reading at the beginning of the meeting should not be over fifteen minutes. Open the meeting either by singing, by praising, or by reading plus pray-reading. It is better to pray-read for fifteen minutes and at the most twenty minutes. Do not go further. If you go further, the long opening kills the remainder of the meeting.

After the pray-reading, sometimes the saints may have the leading to share something. This is good. You must give them the time and the liberty to share something. However, the elders should always be in control of the steering wheel of the car or the rudder of the sailing boat. The elders should always do this, but they should not control the meeting. To control the meeting is one thing, but to keep the steering wheel in your hand is another thing. This means you would not let the car go outside of the lane to get in an accident.

To put the steering wheel or the rudder in your hand you must first get the message into you, and you must get into the message to pick up certain crucial points. During the meeting you have to weigh the situation. If thirty minutes have gone by and it seems that there has been nothing solid to nourish people, you should "put out a dish." To put out a dish means to minister a certain crucial point which is rich, refreshing, enlightening, edifying, and building. In principle, however, you should not occupy the entire remaining time. Just serve the saints one dish and let them continue. See what will come out. Many times something will come out in a very positive way. Then you can observe the meeting for another twenty minutes. If the meeting is going on in a good way, let it continue. If you have some more crucial points do not put them out. You may have some more dishes, but keep them for the next meal, for the next meeting. Let the saints testify freely in a rich way. If the meeting still has not been uplifted after twenty minutes, then you need to minister another crucial point, to serve them with "the top dessert." Sometimes you do not need to serve any dish because the sharings in the meeting are very rich and refreshing. You do not need to annul this kind of rich, refreshing sharing. Rather, you have to pray, "Lord, go ahead. Lord, go ahead." Do not think that you have something. Even if you have something, keep it for the next meeting. In other words, the elders should always be ready to make up the lack in the meeting.

THE ELDERS

Some of the elders may think that this is not easy. This is correct. To be an elder is not so easy. This may encourage some of you to resign. Actually, some of you have to resign. You are like a mother hen occupying the nest without laying any eggs. It is better for you to move out and let some young hen come in to lay some eggs for the children. I am being honest with all of you. We must realize that the Bible does not give us the term of eldership. In the United States the terms for the presidency, the senate, and the congress are clearly defined; the terms are four years, six years, and two years respectively. If you are not very competent in governing, the people may not re-elect you after your term expires. There is no term, however, concerning the eldership in the New Testament. This really bothers me because some elders have been "inaugurated" into the eldership for a life-long term.

If I were occupying the nest without laying any eggs, I surely would go back home to sleep, to rest, or to go to the mountains for some good sightseeing and some fresh air. If I stay on the nest without laying any eggs, I delay the saints. If one hundred saints are under your leadership and you do not lay any eggs, they will get delayed. I do not like to see you moved off the nest, but I would like you to exercise to begin to lay eggs tomorrow. Then everyone will be happy and everyone will be peaceful in the church life. If you are there on the nest without laying eggs for two years, who could be happy? Then you may say, "If I would not be the elder, who would be or who else can be?" If you go away, you would see that some can be an elder. You must consider the real situation. The folks of your family were nearly starved to death without the proper meals being served.

THE NEED TO BE SATURATED WITH THE TRUTH

In principle I hope that you would take my word to help the saints in their personal time to get into the Word and also to bring the church meeting into such a living way and, even more, a rich way. The result will come out in many directions when the saints are saturated with the truth. The

Bible indicates that whenever we are filled up within we will utter something (Eph. 5:18-19). When the saints are filled up within they will speak something. Their utterance may be the preaching of the gospel, the teaching of the truth, or the ministry of life. Even now we may encourage the saints to preach the gospel, teach the truth, and minister life, but they are empty. They have the heart and the desire to speak something, but they have no word to say because they are empty. They are not full. Even if some of you try to preach, you will realize that your preaching is not that full. You may try to teach and discover that your teaching is not that full. You want to minister life to others in your neighborhood, to your cousins, to your relatives and in-laws, but you do not have the riches of life. How then can you minister life to others?

THE PROPER DIET

Therefore, it is basic to have the saints getting into the Word personally every day and to have the entire meeting entering into the truth. Meeting after meeting and week after week you will see the accumulation of the truth go onward. I believe this is the proper way. This proper diet will kill all the germs on the negative side. Then there will be very few problems in the church life because the germs will have been killed. So many saints will be healthy and strong because they received the nourishing diet. This holy Word with the Spirit as the content does everything for the church—it produces the church, builds up the church, heals the wounds, swallows all kinds of darkness, and nourishes, strengthens, and enriches. This is the basic thing. If we could just do this one thing, the church would be wonderful.

EACH ONE HAS

First Corinthians 14:26 tells us that whenever we come together, each has a psalm, a teaching, a revelation, a tongue, or an interpretation. Brother Nee once said in a message that probably most of the seeking readers of the Bible would think that while we are coming together and meeting together, the inspiration from the Spirit comes to us and each one has something. Many understand this verse to mean that while the meeting is going on, the believers have something after the inspiration of the Spirit. Brother Nee said that this was wrong. The predicate does say that this one *has* and that one *has*. However, the predicate does not indicate that you are going to have. It indicates that before coming to the meeting, you have something already. This is just like when you are going to have a love feast. Before coming together the food has already been prepared, and then you come with the food. When the time comes for the feast, each one has something.

THE RESPONSIBILITY OF THE ELDERS AND THE SEEKING ONES

Based upon this principle, all the elders and the seeking ones who bear the real burden of the Lord's testimony should be charged and encouraged to pray much. For instance, let us say that tomorrow night we are going to have a meeting covering Romans 8:9-11. There may be two Life-study messages covering these three verses. All the elders and the seeking ones should get themselves prepared before coming to the meeting. They should read and pray-read the verses and look into the messages to get the crucial points. In every message there are crucial points. They should pick up the crucial points, especially the points concerning the life supply or concerning the unveiling of the truth. These seeking ones, especially the elders, should prepare themselves in this way. Then the meeting begins. You have to keep the meeting open to everybody. Let them function. After ten or fifteen minutes nothing may have come out, which indicates that the attendants are not that rich. There is no need to blame them. The elders and the seeking ones who really bear the responsibility of the Lord's recovery in their locality must make up the lack. We must advise the seeking ones that sometimes they should bear the responsibility to give the meeting a good start, but they should not continue to occupy the entire meeting. They need to strike the match to start the burning, and then keep their hands off the meeting and let others do it. If after ten or fifteen minutes nothing good has come out, then the ones who bear the responsibility, especially the elders, must do it again.

By this way no meeting will be so empty, but every meeting will be a rich meal because it is under the hand of the elders and the seeking ones.

LEAVING THE MEETING TO FORTUNE

If the elders and all the seeking ones come to the meeting without this kind of preparation beforehand, they are leaving the entire meeting to fortune. If you come to the meeting without being prepared you may offer a two second prayer such as, "Lord, have mercy upon us and enrich the meeting, Lord." Actually, you have left the entire meeting to fortune. When you see that nothing good is coming out in the meeting, by that time you will have nothing to minister. This means that all of us have come to a love feast, and nobody cooked anything. Everybody came empty-handed. You have left the love feast to the "god of fortune."

You may say, "Do not say this Brother Lee. Did not the Lord use the five loaves and two small fish to feed five thousand, and still there were twelve baskets left over? Why couldn't the Lord do this?" According to your observation you may feel that I am short of faith and that my ways are too practical. The Apostle Paul, however, had faith, but the real situation forced him to make tents to take care of the needs of himself and of the needs of his co-workers. Did he not have the faith? The Bible never teaches us to have the kind of faith which does not require our labor. This is the teaching of superstition and the teaching of Pentecostalism. They have a kind of faith in which eventually they lie to people and build up false miracles. One brother who was a missionary in Indonesia told us that the so-called changing of water into wine during a revival he attended was a great hoax. We do not need to pretend in this way. The Lord may perform a miracle, but I never heard that in the entire church history the Lord repeated the miracle of the feeding of the five thousand with five loaves and two fish. Also, we see in the book of Acts that the believers had everything in common for a short period of time. This did not work so well for a long time, so when the Apostle Paul came on the scene there was no longer such a practice. You still have to make a living by yourself and work with your own hands. If you do not work, you should not eat (2 Thes. 3:10). To work properly, to gain more so that you can take care of the needy ones, is the proper going on for the long run in the New Testament.

Do not think that to get yourself prepared for the meeting is not scriptural. It is absolutely scriptural, but it depends on what way you prepare. If you go to the concordance and to the Scofield Reference Bible to pick up some points and some verses and put them together to get yourself prepared to give a long message, your message will make everybody sleepy. This will be the best sleeping dose, and this is empty and killing. According to our practice so far, we have the holy Word in our hand and by the Lord's mercy He has given us a publication that always opens up the Word. Why would you not use this? We need to use these two things—the Word and the "opener" to get ourselves prepared.

We cannot expect the entire congregation to prepare in this way. At least, however, we should expect ourselves, the leading ones, the co-workers, and the ones who take care of certain meetings, to prepare for the meeting in such a way. Our responsibility, our obligation, and our duty is to get ourselves prepared for the coming meeting. I believe that if we would practice in this way, every kind of meeting would be rich. It would not be like some of our experience in the past, because in the past nobody actually bore the responsibility. The church meeting actually is the meeting of the elders and all the serving ones. If the elders and all the serving ones get themselves so prepared, the meeting will be rich. When the whole church comes together, this one may have a psalm, that one may have a teaching, and another may have a revelation. They will not have it by instant inspiration, but they will have it by "pre-readiness." You must prepare yourselves before the meeting time. Through our experiences, we have the way to prepare ourselves. To prepare yourself for the meeting is to get into the Word and to get into some messages which can help you to enter into the truth. This will be a rich preparation for you to take care of the meeting, and eventually the meeting will serve a dual purpose—to nourish the saints and, for the long run, to educate the saints.

GROWING GRADUALLY BY LIFE AND BY THE TRUTH

While the issue of nourishment is forever, the nourishment itself only remains temporarily. Once the truth has been constituted into someone, however, it will remain there forever and its remaining is its supply. Our need for the long run is this kind of education with the truth, which is really something solid, living, and existing. We need this. Do not expect to have an overnight success which is like a factory making artificial flowers. Overnight you can produce many flowers, but in a genuine nursery or garden it takes time to grow flowers. Do not pick up the thought that we could do a quick work. You may have the thought that within two years a great number of people will be added to the church. Most of these people, however, may be empty. This is mushrooming. We must take care of the church in a way of growing gradually by life and by truth.

LIVING IN THE SPIRIT AND SPEAKING IN THE SPIRIT

We also must remember that whenever we speak in the meeting, we should speak in the Spirit. Today we are in the New Testament age, but even David in the Old Testament age spoke in the Spirit (2 Sam. 23:2). David's speaking in Spirit was not a kind of inspiration. This is the religious thought. I beg you all to drop this thought of inspiration. Inspiration indicates the degradation of God's people from the living God to a religion. If we serve the living God and this God is the Spirit, we should be in the Spirit all the time if we mean business with Him. Even in the Old Testament times the psalmists and those like David all were living in the Spirit. Therefore, whenever they spoke, they spoke in the Spirit. This does not mean that they were indulging in the flesh like King Saul. He was indulging in the flesh, but God used him to demonstrate something and he received some inspiration. This was Saul, but this was not David.

If we had been working, living, and acting in the Spirit throughout the whole day from morning to evening, when we come to the meeting we will speak in the Spirit. If, however, we are busy with family things, with money, with our bank account, with business, with jobs, and with interviews, our talk to people will not be in the Spirit at all. It is possible that as one of the elders, I could be such a person, but I cannot be absent from the meeting. I have to go there and I have to sit in the front row in order to take care of the responsibility. When you come in the meeting in this way you are not in the Spirit but in death, and your coming in brings in death. This is not the Spirit and not of life. Then you may feel obligated to speak. When you speak something, that kills the meeting or at the very least lowers down the meeting because you are not a person in Spirit.

In 1 Corinthians 7 Paul's speaking concerning dealing with marriage life comprises forty verses. In verse 25 of this long chapter Paul says that he has no commandment of the Lord, but he gives his opinion. In verse 40 he says that what he is speaking is according to his opinion, but he also says, "I think that I also have the Spirit of God." Here is a man telling people his opinion, yet he is still in the Spirit. Whenever such a person opens his mouth, the Spirit comes out. This enlivens the meetings. The same word out of one person's mouth may be a kind of enlightening and life-giving, but out of another person's mouth that word may be a kind of killing. This all depends on whether we live in the Spirit or whether we live in something else. If we do not live in the Spirit yet we expect to have a living meeting, that will be just an opera or a drama. That will be just like something in the theater, a performance with you as a performer. At least a number of times our meetings were just like a drama with no living reality.

Therefore, when you go back to your locality, you must call a meeting, not of all the saints, but at least of all the serving ones who have a heart for the Lord's recovery, to have some fellowship with them to consider and to reconsider the situation. We must have a change. I do not mean that we have to have a radical change, but we must have a kind of advancing change. We should not be contented with our present meeting. This does not mean that our meetings are not good. Comparatively speaking they are quite good, but we are not satisfied.

BEARING THE ARK

The elders and all the serving ones must come together to pray and to fellowship. Every one of these serving ones must be charged, including the elders, to bear the ark of the testimony on their shoulders. This group of faithful ones may be between ten and twenty-five saints. Before every meeting, these dear saints should be living in the Spirit and should get themselves fully ready to bear the ark. The meeting is the ark, the testimony. We need some faithful ones like the Levites to bear the ark. The most devastating thing to me is to come into a meeting with no one bearing the ark. You also must realize that the ark cannot be carried on by one person. There is the need for coordination. To bear the ark needs a team. I came to the meetings a few times with the sensation that no one there was bearing the testimony. There were just performers. The church decided to have a Wednesday meeting and all the elders and serving ones are obligated to come. Then they come without a burden and without the Spirit. They come to pray-read the Word and then to speak something. This is really devastating when no one bears the ark. This kills the appetite for the saints to come to the meetings.

HAVING A TIME WITH THE SERVING ONES

When you elders go back, you must have a time with the serving ones. If the elders make themselves a special, particular group, they are sectarian. They should not be a drop of oil in a bucket of water, but only drops of water. In some churches, however, I noticed that the elders are a drop of oil and could never be blended together with the water. They are a special rank, a special class. You must kill that class and annul that rank. It is a shame among us that there is a class and that there is a rank. If you keep this special class, you should not expect that your meeting will be living. You must be water. What I mean by being just water is that you are not anything in particular. You are just a brother. The church is not yours and the meeting is not yours. The church belongs to the saints and the meetings are the saints' meetings, so you must be one with the saints. Some of the saints are still young, yet a good number have grown up and they are serving and bearing some responsibility. It is better to have a time together with them. Get with them to reconsider how to take care of the church and the church meetings. If you do this, I believe you will see something positive.

CHAPTER TWELVE

BRINGING THE SAINTS INTO THE TRUTH

(4)

USING THE LIFE-STUDY MESSAGES
IN THE CHURCH MEETINGS

Concerning the use of the Life-study messages in the church meetings, the elders in each locality need to seek the Lord's leading as to which book of the New Testament is most helpful to the church at the present time. In making this decision the elders should fellowship with the serving ones in the church. This is a principle the elders need to follow. Instead of making this decision by themselves, the elders should fellowship with those who are interested in bearing responsibility, not only of the church in their locality but also of the Lord's recovery. Such persons, whether brothers or sisters, should be included in the fellowship regarding which New Testament book would be most helpful to the church.

Once the decision has been made concerning which New Testament book to use, you should go on to consider how much time is needed to cover that book. Then you should set up a schedule. For example, suppose you decide to use the book of Ephesians. The *Life-study of Ephesians* has ninety-seven messages. If you take one message a week, you will need almost two years to cover all the messages on Ephesians. If you take two messages a week, you will finish the book in less than a year. I am quite certain that you cannot cover more than one message in a meeting.

The elders also need to consider which verses should be used with a particular message. If you are covering the book of Ephesians, you may want to use only three verses for a particular message. Once you have made a decision concerning verses, you should then assign a certain message with the accompanying verses for a particular meeting. The leading ones need a thorough knowledge of each message and of the basic verses related to the message. This knowledge will include the outline, the central thought, and the crucial points. As long as you have the knowledge of these three matters, it will be easy for you to cover a complete message in one meeting. As a result of having this knowledge, you will know which portions of the message should be emphasized and which portions do not need emphasis, but simply need to be read in order to maintain a good continuation.

I believe that most Life-study messages can be read in thirty minutes. Sometimes in reading messages in a church meeting you may skip over part of a paragraph, or even an entire paragraph, in order to save time. Along with reading the message, you should pray-read the basic verses.

The reading of a Life-study message in a meeting should be considered the same as the speaking of such a message. In other words, the reading of a message should be treated as if it were the actual speaking of that message.

The conducting of a meeting in which a Life-study message is read depends very much on the leading ones. These meetings should be living and uplifted, and the saints must have the opportunity to function. However, the time should not be wasted. Regarding this the leading ones need skill to support and enrich the meeting. Suppose after several minutes nothing living, real, solid, and rich comes forth in fellowship. If this is the situation the elders should minister a "dish" to enrich the "meal."

Reading the Life-study messages in the meetings will be very profitable to the churches. I believe that this is more profitable than the elders using the Life-studies to make messages to give in the meetings. This does not mean that the elders should no longer give such messages. The point here is that reading the Life-study messages is profitable. Reading the message with the proper emphasis will ensure profit to the church. Yet it is also profitable for those who are saturated with the truth to give messages that use certain basic verses and crucial points from the Life-study messages. However, if one is not saturated with the truth, but simply makes a message based upon a Life-study, that will not be as profitable as reading a Life-study message and regarding that reading as the speaking of the message. Of course, you have the liberty to give messages according to your burden and even to call a conference for the purpose of giving such messages.

SPEAKING THE SAME THING

We are here for the Lord's recovery. I am not doing my own work, and you are not doing your own work. We all are bearing one testimony; we all have our shoulders under the "staves" of the "ark." Since we are all bearing the one testimony, we all should speak the same thing (1 Cor. 1:10). But the speaking in certain places is leading the saints in the direction that is away from the Lord's recovery. Such speaking may not be wrong or unscriptural. It may be right and scriptural, but eventually it will lead the saints in a wrong direction.

If we go in a straight line, we shall reach a proper goal. But if our direction is off, eventually we shall reach a goal that is not the goal of the Lord's recovery. Even after a short period of time, trouble may come to the recovery through your way of speaking scriptural things, that is, through your speaking of good messages. Although there is nothing wrong with your speaking, it may lead others in a wrong direction. If so, eventually that will become a problem to the whole recovery.

The recovery is not merely a local matter. Although the recovery is in your local church, the recovery is universal. If you lead those in your locality in a direction that is off from the recovery, then there will be two directions—the direction in the recovery as a whole and the direction in your locality. If you teach in a way that leads others in a different direction, some may receive your teaching, but many of those in the Lord's recovery will reject it. They will not "swallow" your teaching.

From experience we know that the one who teaches differently is the first one to be sacrificed. This means that if you teach differently, you run the risk not of sacrificing the recovery but of sacrificing yourself. We all need to practice Paul's word to Timothy: "Even as I urged you, when I was going into Macedonia, to remain in Ephesus in order that you might charge certain ones not to teach differently" (1 Tim. 1:3). Instead of teaching differently, we should all speak the same thing.

Since I am the one who has given the Life-study messages, it is rather awkward for me to speak about them. However, I can say that the Lord's recovery has been going on by the ministry. If the ministry had not come to this country, the recovery would not be prevailing here. The recovery came through the ministry, and the recovery has been going on by the ministry. If you, then, speak something that is off from the ministry, surely the recovery will not follow that speaking. It is a dream to think that the entire recovery will follow the speaking that is different from that of the ministry. Therefore, if you speak differently, you will exclude yourself from the recovery by your speaking. No one else will exclude you; you will be excluded by your own speaking, concept, and attitude.

It is no doubt true that every local church has its own jurisdiction. However, we have taught very strongly that each local church is not a Body of Christ; all the churches together are the one Body. Because of this, what happens in one place will affect other places. This means that what you do in your locality will affect the other local churches. News travels quickly from one place to another. Also, the saints who are now in your locality later may move to a different locality.

Those who teach differently are not able to stop the ministry in the Lord's recovery. The ministry brought the recovery to this country, and the ministry is still carrying the recovery. How can the ministry receive dissenting teachings? Those who teach differently will cause trouble first to themselves and then to others and to the recovery. They will damage others and then cause damage to the recovery. Such damage is the responsibility of those who teach differently.

We all need to consider what we minister, preach, and teach. This means that we need to take care of all the churches. Before the Lord I can testify that this was my practice in China, and it is my practice today. When I was in China speaking in a certain locality, I considered how the other churches might be affected by my speaking. I asked myself, "Will this cause trouble to the other churches? How will it affect them? Will the entire recovery be able to accept this?" I realized that if I did not consider my speaking in this way, I could cause trouble. I could speak something that the recovery as a whole would not receive. I could speak something that others would reject because it was contrary to their taste.

A TASTE FOR THE MINISTRY

Just as people have different tastes in food, so the Lord's recovery also has a taste for the ministry that has built up the recovery over the years. The recovery was raised up with a certain taste. Those who have been raised with this taste will reject a taste that is contrary to it. This means that if you speak something contrary to the taste of the Lord's recovery, your speaking will be rejected, and you will be the first to suffer loss. We have seen a number of examples of this in the past.

In 1964 I invited a certain brother to share a message in one session each day of a training. That brother's teaching was very good. Otherwise, I would not have asked him to share that training with me. However, the speaking of that brother went against the taste of the saints. One brother told me that this brother's teaching was too philosophical. This indicates that even though the recovery had been in this country less than two years, the saints had already acquired a taste for life.

Concerning a matter such as this, it is useless to argue about who is right and who is wrong. The point here is that saints have a taste, and they do not accept what is contrary to it. Let me give you an illustration of what I mean by a taste for the ministry in the Lord's recovery. One day I encouraged a brother to try eating sea cucumber, a Chinese dish that I enjoy very much. Even though the sea cucumber had been prepared by an expert cook and I had strongly recommended it, the brother refused to eat it, because it was contrary to his taste in food. Likewise, you may think that your speaking is good, but it is not according to the taste in the recovery.

If you are wise you will know the taste of those to whom you are speaking. All the churches in the recovery were raised up through the ministry, and the saints have been "eating" this ministry for years and have a taste for it. Even though no churches have been produced by your speaking, you now begin to "serve" the saints with something different from the ministry, with something that is not according to their taste. If you do this, you will cause trouble for yourself. Just as parents will have trouble with their children if they force them to eat food that is contrary to their taste, so you will have trouble if you expect the saints to "eat" something against the taste in the Lord's recovery.

Those who teach differently are not wise, for they do not know the environment, situation, and condition of the Lord's recovery. The Lord's recovery has been raised up in a particular way. Brothers who teach differently actually are trying to bring in a foreign element; they are trying to wedge in a foreign particle into the "body" of the recovery. The recovery will not accept any kind of foreign element or article. As we have strongly emphasized, the reason is that the saints have their taste.

Although the recovery is not controlled by any person, there is a controlling factor in the Lord's recovery, and this factor is the taste in the recovery. The recovery has a particular taste because it has a certain life that came from its birth. Just as a human being is born with a life that gives him a certain taste, so the Lord's recovery was born with the life that has its own particular taste. This taste is the controlling factor in the Lord's recovery. No one can overthrow this controlling factor. If you try to overthrow it, you yourself will be overthrown. This means that you actually overthrow yourself, causing yourself to be separated from the Lord's recovery.

I do not insist that all the churches use the Life-study messages. However, I wish to point out that this ministry brought the recovery to this country and has been helping and nourishing the recovery. The recovery has grown up with the "food" provided by this ministry. Now it is impossible for the saints to change their taste. If you try to change the taste of the saints, you will be foolish, you will waste your time, and you will cause damage. If you feel that your teaching is better than that in the Lord's recovery, you should serve your "food" to those who have a taste for it. Those who have been raised on certain foods may occasionally eat something different. But for the long run in their daily living they will eat what matches their taste and reject what is contrary to it.

Since this is the situation among the saints in the Lord's recovery, we should be wise to learn the basic truths and then serve these truths to the saints. If we do this, everyone will be happy, and we shall have a peaceful situation not only among individual saints but also between the churches and between the churches and the ministry.

THE NATURE OF THE NEW TESTAMENT MINISTRY

If you can give messages that fit the taste of the Lord's recovery without using the Life-study messages, that would be wonderful. Such messages will be profitable to the recovery. messages that fit the taste of the recovery are truly part of the New Testament ministry. No one should think that only what I minister is the New Testament ministry. Paul, of course, ministered the New Testament ministry. Martin Luther also ministered a part of the New Testament ministry. Many among us also minister the ministry of the New Testament.

Whatever we minister must be of the nature of the New Testament ministry. Whether or not a particular ministry is part of the New Testament ministry can be proved by applying three governing principles: one, the principle of the processed Triune God being dispensed into His chosen people; second, the principle of Christ and the church; and third, the principle of Christ, the Spirit, life, and the church. If your teaching can pass this threefold test, your teaching is part of the New Testament ministry. Any ministry that is part of the New Testament ministry will be welcomed by the saints in the Lord's recovery. Any other ministry, however, will only cause trouble for the recovery.

THE APPOINTMENT OF ELDERS

If a brother is to be an adequate elder, or even an adequate leader in any church meeting, he needs to have the adequate knowledge of the truth. Anyone who does not have this knowledge of the truth cannot take care of the church, God's flock, in a proper way. If you would be a leader in the church caring for the flock, and if you would keep spiritual germs away from the church life, you must have an adequate knowledge of the New Testament truths. As a help to gaining the full knowledge of the basic truths, I would encourage you to go through the entire New Testament using the Recovery Version with the notes and the Life-studies. According to a rough estimate, if a person spends two hours a day studying the New Testament in this way, he can go through the entire New Testament in five years.

Recently a brother raised a question concerning the appointment of elders. A person is born a human being and remains a human being permanently. No matter what kind of human being a person may be, he remains a human being. The appointment of elders is different. Anyone who desires to be an elder permanently should resign, and whenever a brother realizes that he is not qualified to be in the eldership, he should also resign.

In Acts 20:28 we have a word concerning the appointing of elders (overseers) by the Holy Spirit. We may say that here we have the divine appointment of elders to take care of the flock of God. However, I do not believe that all those who are elders in the church today are divinely appointed. Some have become elders in a natural way, perhaps because they were the first one in their locality, or because the church in their place was raised up through them. But who can tell such a brother that he should not be an elder? My purpose in saying this is not to disappoint anyone; my purpose is to present the situation in an honest way.

When some hear that certain brothers have become elders in a natural way, they may say, "Brother Lee, why don't you do something about this?" My answer to this question is that I do not feel free to do anything. This is one reason I can testify that I do not control any church or any person. I care only to help the churches. I may realize that the appointment of a particular brother as an elder is not a divine appointment, but as I consider the situation I also realize that there is no way to do anything about it. Actually, we all need to humble ourselves and not regard our being an elder as divine. It is very possible that you have become an elder in some way other than that of a divine appointment.

Let us humble ourselves and realize that we are nothing. Others may regard me as something, but I do not consider myself to be anything. I have simply acted according to my conscience and have done the works I felt burdened to do. Let the Lord judge the nature of these works. As Paul says, "For I am conscious of nothing against myself; but I am not justified by this; but He who examines me is the Lord. Therefore do not judge anything before the time, until the Lord comes, who shall both bring to light the hidden things of darkness and make manifest the counsels of the hearts, and then there will be praise to each one from God" (1 Cor. 4:4-5).

Please do not think that your being an elder is a divine appointment. My intention in saying this is that we would all humble ourselves, not claiming to have the assurance that you have been divinely appointed to be elders.

Whether or not you have been divinely appointed to be an elder does not depend on your thought, or someone else's confirmation; it depends on how much you have been constituted of the divine knowledge of the basic New Testament truths. The more you are constituted of the truths of the New Testament, the more you have been divinely appointed to be an elder. Today the divine appointment is nothing other than the adequate knowledge of the basic truths of the New Testament.

We are short of those constituted with the New Testament truths. The churches are somewhat weak simply because of the shortage of brothers who have the adequate knowledge of the basic truths of the New Testament. It would be a great help for a church to have even one such brother.

I would encourage you not to consider whether you have been divinely appointed to be an elder. Some in the Pentecostal movement claim to have a divine appointment, but the result of their so-called appointment is confusion. Others, by contrast, have become saturated with the New Testament truths. Those who are constituted even to some extent of the biblical truths are a great blessing to the church. Wherever they are they are a blessing as they simply live among the saints. They may not have the title or the position of an elder, but as long as they are present in a locality, the church receives the benefit. This is surely a divine appointment.

Do not think that according to my feeling the situation of the elders in all the churches is right. On the contrary, there are situations that I am not happy with. But I would not do anything to change those situations. Nevertheless, I have been falsely accused of being an "autonomous dictator." However, the reason I have not done anything to adjust the situation in certain churches is not that I am afraid of being called a pope or a dictator; the reason is that I realize that such a thing would not be helpful to the church. It would be more profitable to the churches to do nothing about the situation than to do something.

My purpose in speaking concerning the divine appointment of elders is to point out our shortage. Our shortage is the adequate knowledge of the biblical truths. Any brother who becomes an elder should know at least fifty percent of the basic truths of the New Testament. I must tell you honestly that some of those in the position of elders know even less than five percent of the basic truths of God's economy. But who can put these brothers out of the eldership? No one can do this. Furthermore, if these brothers were asked to resign, they would be disappointed.

Once again I wish to emphasize the fact that being an elder does not depend on a human appointment. Rather, being an elder depends on the degree to which one has the proper knowledge of the New Testament economy.

At present, the best way to gain the knowledge of God's New Testament economy is to use the Recovery Version with the notes and the Life-study messages. Do not think that my intention in saying this is to promote my materials. I am simply telling you honestly what is the best way to be constituted of the New Testament truths.

It is difficult to gain from the writings of expositors the adequate knowledge of the basic truths of the New Testament.

The reason is that those writings were not put out with this intention or burden. On the contrary, those writings, composed for scholarship, are in a different category and may actually hinder you from receiving the knowledge of the basic truths.

Again I say, if you would be qualified to be an elder and take care of the church, you need to be constituted of the New Testament truths. If you do not have this divine deposit in your being, you are not qualified for the eldership, because you lack the necessary "capital."

Those who are not constituted of the truth may be able to bring people into the church life, but they are not able to take them on. One day, a certain person said to me, "Brother Lee, I can only bring people into the church. I am not able to give them nourishment and to build them up." I replied, "Brother, it is very good that you realize this. I hope that you will not go beyond the matter of bringing people in. Do not try to go further. Let others do a further work on the saints." However, this brother's actual practice was very different. Because he did not have an adequate knowledge of the truth, he was not qualified to be an elder. To be sure, he was not divinely appointed as an elder.

Who is the one divinely appointed to be an elder? Again, I would say that the one who is divinely appointed is the one who knows at least a major part of the New Testament truths. This is his qualification and also his capital. Furthermore, I again encourage you to gain this capital by using the Recovery Version with the notes and the Life-study messages. I would also ask you to seek a way to help the saints in your locality to use these rich materials. This will be a great profit to all the churches.

CHAPTER THIRTEEN

BRINGING THE SAINTS INTO THE TRUTH

(5)

OUR HISTORY

In this chapter I would like to say something further concerning our experiences from the past years until today. We surely have learned much from our past history. I was with the Brethren Assembly for seven and a half years and I was a very faithful attendant of their meetings. They always centered on typology, prophecy, dispensation, and exhortations to good conduct. I took down notes and studied all their publications. I also put many points into my old Chinese Bibles which are full of notes. Undoubtedly, I received something from them.

Then the Lord brought me from that Brethren situation into the Lord's recovery. At that time our church life was wholly dependent upon Brother Nee's messages. He first published twenty-four volumes of his paper which was called *The Christian*. That became a great help for us—the honest and sincere learners. We all treasured those twenty-four volumes and to some extent the messages conveyed in those twenty-four volumes got into our being. I can testify that this was so with me. I was able to present these messages in a doctrinal way in any place, at any time, and to any person who needed the truth. I could present them, not in a common way, but in a way of teaching them to pass on to others.

Brother Nee was very busy in those days and he was not so healthy. He always needed some kind of rest year round because he had a heart problem. It was very hard for him to give us conferences often. From 1932 through 1949 in the

eighteen years I was with him, he gave not more than ten conferences. It was from 1940 through 1942 that Brother Nee
carried out his burden to have a long training. He did his best
to hold conferences during those two to three years mainly for
the trainees' sake. Those conferences were part of his training
given to us. During those two or three years he would have a
few days for a conference about every two months, but most of
those messages were not printed.

Also, the atmosphere among the saints in the Lord's recovery in those days was that the general attendants merely
came to listen to messages to get inspiration. Very few of the
saints took notes. The messages which Brother Nee gave were
good messages and were very touching, rich, uplifting, living, and refreshing. Of course, there was much inspiration
in these messages, so all who attended these meetings were
excited. They received the help and they were happy, but they
only retained inspiration. When there was a need to present
the truths in Brother Nee's messages to others, very few were
capable of doing this. This has caused me to consider our situation very much. I realize the need to release the truth for the
producing of the churches, for the bringing up, for the edifying, and for the building up of the churches. I surely have
been cautioned by the situation in Brother Nee's time. As far
as the attendants of his meetings were concerned, his messages were good for inspiration and the ministry of life to
help the saints to grow in life, but the saints did not have the
view of being built up in the truth so they could continue to
present the same truths to the needy ones.

Even among the co-workers at that time, only a few out of
five hundred co-workers could present a truth in a doctrinal
way. For example, Brother Nee shared a number of times on
the truth of sanctification, and he made this truth very doc-
trinally clear. We all received the help in life through the
inspiration of these particular messages. After we received
the help in life, however, we did not retain much of the truth
in our memory. Actually, we were not trained to present this
truth to others, so most of the co-workers were not capable of
teaching others by presenting the truth in an adequate way.
This was the reason that, among us, only the works of three

brothers were printed: Brother Nee's books, Dr. Yu's translations of the mystical books such as the autobiography of Madame Guyon, and a small portion of my books. This was the extent of the publishing work in China. Of course, I always preached what Brother Nee preached and taught. I was also very much occupied with the churches, so I had no thought of publishing books. I was fully occupied with the work, with the burden to take care of the churches.

When we came to Taiwan this afforded us a new environment to reconsider how to meet the need. First, I had a series of messages which I called "The Principle Truths of the Scriptures" within the year of 1949. That laid a very good foundation for the work in Taiwan. Some of you are still using these lessons. Through that I learned that to give messages for conferences could help the saints to grow in life very much, but that would not help the saints to be built up in the full knowledge of the truth. In 1 Timothy 2:4 Paul tells Timothy that God desires all men to be saved and to come to the full knowledge of the truth. I realized that to have conferences or messages given on the Lord's Day would surely not be adequate enough to build up the saints in the full knowledge of the truth.

From 1950 through 1961 we had three to four months of training every year. In every period of training there was always an item of the study of the Bible. The first book that we studied in this kind of training was Ephesians. In 1953 a book in Chinese was published with these messages on the book of Ephesians. Since 1954 I began to use the term Life-study. I used this word the first time for a general study of the entire Bible. We had a long period of training for about six months in which we received a general view of the New Testament and also a part of the Old Testament. Many saints became excited about this. These messages laid a very good foundation on the island of Taiwan.

I still discovered that even by that way not many saints in Taiwan could present the truth as it should be presented. I left Taiwan at the end of 1961 and I stayed in the United States for four years. From 1965 I went back to Taiwan about once every two years to hold a conference. Since 1961 in

Taiwan there has not been this kind of training based upon the biblical truths, so this has left a situation of a lack of training in Taiwan.

During my first ten years in the United States I only held conferences plus summer trainings. I did not have the time to train the saints in the biblical knowledge. Then I realized that this was not adequate. The conferences mainly were to pick up a certain burden or an item and give anywhere from seven to ten messages. The messages in the conferences mainly impressed people with the point of life and rendered them some inspiration. However, this never performed an adequate job of building up the saints in the biblical education concerning Christ, the Spirit, life, and the church. Due to this I began to consider that we needed annual trainings to go through the entire New Testament. Eventually, I intended not only to go through the New Testament, but also in the mean time to go through the Old Testament. As a result, we began with the two lines of the Old and New Testaments.

THE ANNUAL TRAININGS

I am very happy about these annual trainings because many truths were not put out according to inspiration, but according to the books of the Bible. The speaking in a conference just depends upon the speaker's burden. A series of messages are given to release that burden and all these messages cover certain points. They do not, however, serve the purpose of educating the saints or building up the saints in the full knowledge of the truth. To study our way through the books of the Bible, however, does not allow us to pick up our burden to put out something in the way of inspiration. Rather, it forces us and even regulates us in the line of the truth according to the divine revelation. For instance, in Matthew there is the basic truth of the kingdom of the heavens. I do not believe that any conference speaker would pick up a burden with an inspiration to speak about the truth of the kingdom of the heavens. This would be very rare. When you make a decision to cover all the books of the New Testament, though, you cannot avoid covering the truth in its entirety.

I must truthfully testify that if I had not been writing the notes on the books of the Bible, I would never have had an inspiration to give messages on the book of Mark. I do not believe any burden would have come to me to give a conference concerning the books of Mark or James. In the first eleven years I was in the United States, all the messages I gave were concerning Christ, the Spirit, the human spirit, the ground of the church, and the Trinity. I even very rarely quoted anything from the book of Mark. When we came to Mark in the Life-study of the Bible, I was wondering what I was going to write. I had no choice and I was forced to write something. According to my realization, however, the trainings on the Epistles of Peter, the Epistles of John, and the books of Mark and James were in the heavens. The best trainings were these trainings. The light came just by my being forced to write the notes on these books.

I was never so clear about 1 John as I was during the training on this book. I still have a clear bird's-eye view of 1 John. The subject of this book is the fellowship of the divine life. It is divided into three parts: the fellowship of the divine life (1:1—2:11), the teaching of the divine anointing (2:12-27), and the virtues of the divine birth (2:28—5:21). The virtues of the divine birth comprise three items: to practice the divine right-eousness (2:28—3:10a), to practice the divine love (3:10b—5:3), and to overcome the world, death, sin, the Devil, and idols (5:4-21). This is a bird's-eye view of the wonderful book of 1 John.

According to my consideration, the best of all the trainings we have had was the one on the book of Mark. This exceeded all the others. If I was not compelled to get into Mark, I would have never touched it. This shows that we are partial in our studying of the Bible. We are not balanced, but by studying the books of the Bible in a definite way we have no choice. Every book is God-breathed so we must study them.

THE NEED TO BE EDUCATED
IN THE FULL KNOWLEDGE OF THE TRUTH

Despite all the trainings we have given covering the entire New Testament, I realize that still the saints in the Lord's recovery in the United States have not been helped to be so knowledgeable of the truth. In other words, they have not been helped to come into the full knowledge of the truth. I discovered that even many of the positive ones in the Lord's recovery cannot present the truth. For example, many of the saints in the Lord's recovery are not able to present the matter of sanctification clearly to people in a doctrinal way. All the saints in the Lord's recovery need to be those who preach the gospel, teach the truth, and minister life to others. I discovered that so many dear saints have the heart to do this, yet when they begin to preach, teach, or minister life, they have nothing to say. They have nothing as the gospel, the good news to impart something to others. They have the desire to teach the truth, but they do not have the materials constituted into their being to talk about. Many saints treasure the ground of the church. They would tell people, "We are standing on the church ground. If you do not have this, you will be divisive." When the other people ask what the church ground is, many of the saints have little to say. The outsiders do not know what the ground of the church is, and neither do many of us know.

A person may be attending a denomination for twenty years. Eventually he is not able to preach even a little of the gospel because he was not trained or raised up in that way. Many have been sitting in the pews of denominations for every Sunday morning service for over twenty years. Eventually, after twenty years they cannot teach people about one spiritual subject. Our concept when we were there in the denominations was that it was not our obligation to teach. That was not our duty, but that was the duty of the preachers or of the pastors. We never had the thought of being able to teach others. Even in our homes we could not teach our own children. We just encouraged them to go to the service. This principle is nearly the same with us. Most of the saints have been sitting with us for years appreciating all the messages as a treasure. Through all the ministry of the Word they received the help point by point, but they are not capable in presenting the items of the truth to others. We must admit that here we have a great lack and a failure.

I did say in the past that everyone can be an apostle, but

if you do not have the knowledge of the biblical truths, how could you be an apostle? Also, to be an elder you must be appointed by the divine truth. Until you have the knowledge of the divine truth you are not adequate or qualified to be an elder. Even the elders in most of the churches cannot present the truth adequately. We must see that we are short in this matter. If all of the approximately eight thousand saints in the Lord's recovery in the United States would be educated in this way, we would have eight thousand apostles preaching, teaching, and ministering the divine truths. The actual situation, however, is not like this today, so I think we have to wake up.

THE MEETINGS—EDUCATIONAL CENTERS

I am not fellowshipping in a legal way, but in principle I beg the elders to reconsider the way to carry out the meetings. We must have a very available way to carry out God's purpose. We cannot go the religious way. Even today our way of meeting is still very much governed and influenced by the religious way. We come together to pray, read some verses of the Bible, give some messages, and the people who have been sitting in our meetings for years eventually only get some kind of inspiration. This is better than nothing, but for the long run the Lord could not carry out His purpose in this way.

We cannot take the old way of our meeting life. If we continue to take our old way, I am afraid after another ten years we will be in the same condition. We are just giving people a little injection to help them grow in life mainly by inspiration, but no solid truth has been constituted into their being that can remain in their memory and that can be presented to others in a proper doctrinal way. By taking the way we have taken, we have lost the nature of the testimony of Jesus which must be a constitution of the proper truth that produces a proper daily living. If the saints are not properly constituted with the truth, they cannot live a proper life. If they only live by inspiration and not by the constitution of the truth, I do not trust in that kind of living to be a testimony of the Lord.

I feel that we must endeavor to make all the church

meetings educational centers to build the saints up with the proper knowledge. Our meetings should not merely be a restaurant to feed the children or a hospital to heal people. If the parents of a child would not care for the education of their children until they become ten years old, their children would grow up to be persons who are not very useful to society. Proper parents must take care of bringing their children up through elementary, junior high, high school, and college. In like manner, we must educate our spiritual children. We should not only help them grow in life, but also help them to be educated and built up in the proper knowledge of the truth. To carry out this educational work we must come to the Life-study messages with the Recovery Version and the notes. If all the saints could go through the entire New Testament and the Life-studies with the Recovery Version and the notes in five years I would worship the Lord. This would be wonderful.

FULL-TIME YOUNG PEOPLE

There is also a need among us for many young people to dedicate two years to the Lord after graduation from college. These young people who are full-time should spend four hours in the morning to study the Word. Every morning for five days a week they must get into the New Testament from Matthew through Revelation. They should study book after book and chapter after chapter with no choice for a particular book of their preference. They should go directly to the book of Matthew and study their way through the entire New Testament to the end of the book of Revelation with the help of the Recovery Version with its notes and the Life-studies. Hopefully within two years they could finish their study of the entire New Testament. In addition to these four hours of study in the morning, in the afternoon they could pray and have some fellowship and in the evening they could go to meetings or go to the campus for the work there. This would be wonderful if many of our young people could give two years to the Lord in this kind of way. It would be wonderful if there would be a number of young saints in each locality who were fully educated in the basic truth of the entire New Testament.

They will be the foundation and they will teach others. After they are married, they will teach their children.

ENDEAVORING TO GET INTO THE TRUTH

Also, the elders have to endeavor to get into the truth. Do not excuse yourself by saying that you are too old. Even at the age of eighty I spend a certain time every day in the Word. If I can make it, so can you. It all depends upon whether or not we have the heart. We all know the universal proverb which says, "If there is the will, there is the way." All of us elder brothers need to get ourselves saturated, soaked, and constituted with this basic knowledge of God's Word. I must testify that I love God's Word. God is Spirit and God is life. The Spirit is in the Word and the Word is life.

It is not too much for me to propose such a thing strongly. I propose that you study the Bible with an opener, with a help. All of us who have some experience with the Life-study messages know that they may be considered as the best help. They are the most availing and prevailing key to open up the New Testament to all of us. We must remember that at the beginning of any endeavor we always feel awkward and not so successful. However, we must realize that the beginning is the experimental stage, and if we keep endeavoring to get into the truth, I believe the result that will issue will be very promising.

A PRIVATE TIME IN THE LORD'S WORD

We should encourage the saints to have a private time in the Lord's Word and that they should do this as a proper rule of their daily life. Regardless of how busy or how tired we are, we can reserve thirty minutes a day for a time with the Lord in the Word. It all depends upon our will. If there is the will, there is the way. To save half an hour among twenty-four hours is not a hard thing. If the saints could practice one hour or more in the Lord's Word this would be wonderful, but at least we should encourage them to give a half an hour to the Lord every day. The saints should be encouraged to separate or sanctify thirty minutes every day to the Lord. We all can realize what a blessing this will be, and I believe this will make the Lord very pleased. Then every local church needs to find a way to carry out the meetings in the principle of giving the saints the proper education in the full knowledge of the truth.

THE SALVATION OF THE SOUL

The truth concerning the salvation of the soul is contained in a textbook we have published entitled *God's Full Salvation*. Over sixty years ago Brother Nee taught the things concerning the salvation of the soul. I received this teaching and I believed in it, but I could not teach it adequately because I did not know much about it. As a result, I began to study. At that time there were no other books from which I could get any help in this matter. Just by studying the Bible, I had no key to help me to understand what the salvation of the soul was. When I was with the Brethren for seven and a half years, I never had this kind of concept. I could not get any books to help me in this matter, so I had to go back to Brothers Nee's books. Even in his books there were not that many messages, so I had to endeavor. Eventually, I learned how to present this matter. Very few of the Chinese saints who received a great amount of help through Brother Nee's ministry could present a message on the salvation of the soul. We have covered the salvation of the soul quite often and have published many pages on this matter with many points. We must ask ourselves, though, if we are able to present an adequate message on the salvation of the soul. It seems that we all heard this and probably we all knew this, but when we try to present it we cannot make it.

A CHURCH FAMILY TRAINING

I believe that the textbook entitled *God's Full Salvation* will be useful not only for the summer school with the junior high and high school students but also for a weekly church training. There is no need for us to add another meeting for the truth. We have a sufficient number of meetings. It is preferable to have two meetings on the Lord's Day. The Lord's Day morning is the time for us to come together around the Lord's Word for the preaching of the gospel, the teaching of the truth, or for the ministry of life. The Lord's Day evening is always the right time for us to have the Lord's table. One evening a week should be used for the prayer meeting and another evening to gather together around the Lord's Word again. For the long run we should keep such a principle. To have less meetings than this would not be adequate and to have more than this would be quite heavy. In addition to these main meetings, there are also small meetings such as the young people's meeting and children's meeting.

It is possible for us to reserve thirty minutes in both the prayer meeting and the Lord's table meeting to train the saints in the truth. For example, we could pray from 7:30 to 8:30 in the evening, and then from 8:30 to 9:00 p.m. we could have a lesson in the truth. I believe that one hour of prayer is adequate. It would be good if we could use the last half hour of the prayer meeting for a regular church training, which could be called a church family training. We need approximately one hour and fifteen minutes for the Lord's table and then about thirty minutes for the saints to share. The last half hour of the Lord's table should be devoted to another training, which could be called a church family training. We could spend half an hour twice a week using the materials from *God's Full Salvation*. We can train our family just like the mothers daily read some books to their children.

If the elders would give these types of lessons twice a week, this would impress the saints and build them up in the knowlodge of the truth. We could possibly cover the entire textbook of *God's Full Salvation* within one year. Of course, if we are going to carry out this proposal, all the elders need to be "reduced." The best way for the elders to get reduced is to carry out the Lord's work in this way. You must labor. Do not think that it is enough to take the summer school textbook and read it to the saints. That does not work. You must get into it.

THE ISSUE OF TRAINING

I believe the issue of this kind of training will be quite promising. Through this kind of training, most of the saints would be filled with the knowledge of the truth. When they need to talk to people about the gospel, they will have the utterance, the expression, and the material. They will not need to prepare anything. When the need comes, they will be able to teach the saved ones the truth. When the time comes they will also be able to minister life to the seeking Christians who do not meet with us. They will also be enabled to preach the gospel to the unsaved. Then it will be easy for the church to encourage all the saints in the offices, in the schools, in the neighborhoods, and among their relatives, to either preach the gospel, teach the truth, or minister life. This will be the living testimony of the Lord Jesus.

We do not need to be concerned about the number of people we bring in. I would say a strong word—do not proselyte. We need to be those preaching the gospel, teaching the truth, and ministering life to people. The way that others would take as far as the church is concerned is according to their own choice. However, we will show to all the people and especially to the Christian community that we are a group of people full of the knowledge of the divine truths. This will be a strong testimony.

I believe that this is what is on the Lord's heart for His up-to-date recovery. Just for us to meet properly, to stand on the unique ground, and to have a so-called church life without such a prevailing testimony shining out from within us would not make the Lord happy concerning His recovery. We must give the Lord a way to have a recovery full of life and full of the knowledge of the truth so that we can be those preaching the gospel, teaching the truth, and ministering life. If we become constituted with the truth, when we open up our mouth our preaching will be rich. It will not be rich in stories, jokes, or even in so-called biblical doctrines, but rich in Christ, in the Spirit, in life, and in the church. We do have the way to carry this out, because we have the Word. The Word is the conveyer which conveys the gospel, the truth, and life.

Do not be concerned with the spreading of the churches. I do not mean that we should not migrate to other localities. We must migrate, not in the religious, natural way, but by the way of the growth in life and in the truth. We all need to grow in life and in truth gradually. This seems very slow, but actually it will not be slow. This is a propagation, a multiplication, of life. We need something to grow with so we are growing in life and we are growing with the truth. Then we will be the kind of people who live in the way of preaching, teaching, and ministering to others wherever we are. Whether we have one hundred meeting in our locality or one thousand, it is about the same. Whether there are ten churches in your area or just five, we do not need to be bothered. Be assured, however, that if we live such a life there will surely be an increase, not by human doings or by human effort, but by the growth in life and the knowledge of the truth.

GROCERIES FOR THE CHURCHES AND THE SAINTS

In the past ten years what the ministry has done is to produce the groceries for the churches and the saints. We must realize that the quantity of the groceries will always be much greater than the eating capability. If this were not the case, a morning might come when you would have nothing to eat. Years ago we probably went to our "refrigerator" and there was nothing there, and we went to our "shelves" and they were empty. This is not the case today. Today on our church shelves there are many groceries. The only problem is that some of these groceries have been frozen in your refrigerator for five years. We should not be bothered by the quantity of the groceries. We need to measure and weigh what our present need is to decide what particular groceries can meet the need in our locality.

THE TORTOISE WINS THE RACE

A diligent seeker of the Lord could possibly finish the entire New Testament by studying two hours a day for two and a half years. If the church, however, took seven and a half years to get through the entire New Testament this would still be wonderful. Never forget the race between the hare and the tortoise. The tortoise wins the race. If we keep going slowly, we will win the race. All the "running ones" will be defeated, but the working ones will win the race. We need to eat regularly, continuously, and slowly. I advise you not to go too fast, but to go slowly. You will then reach the goal. If we had started this practice ten years ago, we would have finished the entire New Testament already. Even if you get through half of the New Testament, you will see that you are different. Also, if the entire church could get through half of the New Testament, the church would be different.

ABOUT THE AUTHOR

Witness Lee was born in 1905 in northern China and raised in a Christian family. At age 19 he was fully captured for Christ and immediately consecrated himself to preach the gospel for the rest of his life. Early in his service, he met Watchman Nee, a renowned preacher, teacher, and writer. Witness Lee labored together with Watchman Nee under his direction. In 1934 Watchman Nee entrusted Witness Lee with the responsibility for his publication operation, called the Shanghai Gospel Bookroom.

Prior to the Communist takeover in 1949, Witness Lee was sent by Watchman Nee and his other co-workers to Taiwan to ensure that the things delivered to them by the Lord would not be lost. Watchman Nee instructed Witness Lee to continue the former's publishing operation abroad as the Taiwan Gospel Bookroom, which has been publicly recognized as the publisher of Watchman Nee's works outside China. Witness Lee's work in Taiwan manifested the Lord's abundant blessing. From a mere 350 believers, newly fled from the mainland, the churches in Taiwan grew to 20,000 in five years.

In 1962 Witness Lee felt led of the Lord to come to the United States, settling in California. During his 35 years of service in the U.S., he ministered in weekly meetings and weekend conferences, delivering several thousand spoken messages. Much of his speaking has since been published as over 400 titles. Many of these have been translated into over fourteen languages. He gave his last public conference in February 1997 at the age of 91.

He leaves behind a prolific presentation of the truth in the Bible. His major work, *Life-study of the Bible,* comprises over 25,000 pages of commentary on every book of the Bible from the perspective of the believers' enjoyment and experience of God's divine life in Christ through the Holy Spirit. Witness Lee was the chief editor of a new translation of the New Testament into Chinese called the Recovery Version and directed the translation of the same into English. The Recovery Version also appears in a number of other languages. He provided an extensive body of footnotes, outlines, and spiritual cross references. A radio broadcast of his messages can be heard on Christian radio stations in the United States. In 1965 Witness Lee founded Living Stream Ministry, a non-profit corporation, located in Anaheim, California, which officially presents his and Watchman Nee's ministry.

Witness Lee's ministry emphasizes the experience of Christ as life and the practical oneness of the believers as the Body of Christ. Stressing the importance of attending to both these matters, he led the churches under his care to grow in Christian life and function. He was unbending in his conviction that God's goal is not narrow sectarianism but the Body of Christ. In time, believers began to meet simply as the church in their localities in response to this conviction. In recent years a number of new churches have been raised up in Russia and in many eastern European countries.

OTHER BOOKS PUBLISHED BY
Living Stream Ministry

Titles by Witness Lee:

Abraham—Called by God	0-7363-0359-6
The Experience of Life	0-87083-417-7
The Knowledge of Life	0-87083-419-3
The Tree of Life	0-87083-300-6
The Economy of God	0-87083-415-0
The Divine Economy	0-87083-268-9
God's New Testament Economy	0-87083-199-2
The World Situation and God's Move	0-87083-092-9
Christ vs. Religion	0-87083-010-4
The All-inclusive Christ	0-87083-020-1
Gospel Outlines	0-87083-039-2
Character	0-87083-322-7
The Secret of Experiencing Christ	0-87083-227-1
The Life and Way for the Practice of the Church Life	0-87083-785-0
The Basic Revelation in the Holy Scriptures	0-87083-105-4
The Crucial Revelation of Life in the Scriptures	0-87083-372-3
The Spirit with Our Spirit	0-87083-798-2
Christ as the Reality	0-87083-047-3
The Central Line of the Divine Revelation	0-87083-960-8
The Full Knowledge of the Word of God	0-87083-289-1
Watchman Nee—A Seer of the Divine Revelation ...	0-87083-625-0

Titles by Watchman Nee:

How to Study the Bible	0-7363-0407-X
God's Overcomers	0-7363-0433-9
The New Covenant	0-7363-0088-0
The Spiritual Man 3 volumes	0-7363-0269-7
Authority and Submission	0-7363-0185-2
The Overcoming Life	1-57593-817-0
The Glorious Church	0-87083-745-1
The Prayer Ministry of the Church	0-87083-860-1
The Breaking of the Outer Man and the Release ...	1-57593-955-X
The Mystery of Christ	1-57593-954-1
The God of Abraham, Isaac, and Jacob	0-87083-932-2
The Song of Songs	0-87083-872-5
The Gospel of God 2 volumes	1-57593-953-3
The Normal Christian Church Life	0-87083-027-9
The Character of the Lord's Worker	1-57593-322-5
The Normal Christian Faith	0-87083-748-6
Watchman Nee's Testimony	0-87083-051-1

Available at
Christian bookstores, or contact Living Stream Ministry
2431 W. La Palma Ave. • Anaheim, CA 92801
1-800-549-5164 • www.livingstream.com